MARKETS
AND
MARKET LOGIC

ISBN 0-941275-00-0
Printed in the United States of America
First Edition
Book Design by Shi Yung

MARKETS
AND
MARKET LOGIC

J. Peter Steidlmayer and Kevin Koy

The Porcupine Press, Chicago

To the trekker, Africa, 1984.

— J. Peter Steidlmayer

To those who push the third quarter.

-- Kevin Koy

CONTENTS

CONTENTS

I. The Market's Principles

1

INTRODUCTION OF PURPOSE

A problem exists in today's civilized world which transcends talk of trading, investing or any pursuit of material gain whatever. With civilization, something very integral to the individual's ability and hence his potential for success and personal satisfaction has been lost. It involves the method man has for acquiring knowledge, which impacts his ability to confidently generate decisions.

In less civilized societies of the past, man fed and clothed himself, defended himself from the elements and his aggressors, and was in virtually every way forced to be self-reliant. His very survival depended on his ability to generate decisions, based on his knowledge combined with his understanding of the current situation. To gain knowledge he observed, recorded, and organized his existence and reality, then drew logical conclusions. In other words, his self-reliance and ability to generate sound decisions came from his knowledge, which in turn came from his own personal experience, his exposure to reality over time. Thus, man's decision-making was once a direct outgrowth of his experience. And as he continually generated sound decisions, his confidence in his ability to interpret reality and react accordingly grew.

In the modern age, society's concept of knowledge does not come primarily from observing reality. It comes from exposure to classroom education, learning from the teachings of instructors and authors. Knowledge — and society's presumption of an individual's ability to generate sound decisions — rests with that individual's exposure to formal classroom education and inculcation in society. This is particularly true in the study of finance and market behavior where laboratory experimentation is not part of the normal curriculum. Yet, what is taught in the classroom often has no basis in practical reality. In other words, experience is discounted. This means that modern man's knowledge — and the manner in which society measures his assumed decision-making abilities — often has no basis in reality. In civilized society, man is not continually forced to think for himself.

Thus, today we have two forms of knowledge: that which comes directly as a result of one's own observation of reality, and that which comes from a derivative source such as a teacher, a book, a television show or movie, etc. The first form was all that man had prior to the introduction of sophisticated forms of communication. The second form modern man relies on heavily, often at the expense of being correct and accurate.

The problem that comes from relying on the second form of knowledge is illustrated in what has been promulgated about organized markets. Most of what has been written and promoted, while generally accepted as correct, is illogical. (Surprisingly little published information has been compared to reality, thought through and revised.) Because of this discounting of exposure to, and observation of, market reality, little has been published which conceptualizes and develops a sound trading and investing understanding and approach. Until now, only one of the two possible logical approaches to organized futures, options, and stock markets has been advanced. This was presented in *Securities Analysis,* the groundbreaking work of Benjamin Graham and William Dodd. Graham and Dodd assumed that price and value were not necessarily equal in organized markets, and advocated that investors study fundamental (outside the market) information to locate situations where price was below value. To our knowledge, until now, no work has been published which has gone beyond Graham and Dodd to correctly specify how markets, particularly organized markets, function in reality, and how a person, once he understands the market, can put the odds of success in his favor to a considerable extent.

Markets and Market Logic will present knowledge, but knowledge which is not distilled by what has been previously taught. The knowledge presented in this book is drawn directly from experience. Unfortunately, now that this knowledge is put in book form, it becomes part of the second category, knowledge once removed.

It is therefore important for each reader to go beyond this book. Observe, reflect and analyze what is put forth herein as reality in markets familiar to you, and think for yourself. This should be feasible, since knowledge provided in this book will build upon each reader's own experience. This book will demonstrate that all markets act alike, a concept which should be understood by consumers who have practical exposure to everyday markets.

This is not to say that the knowledge and concepts introduced herein will be easy to embrace and apply. Indeed, they are expected to be very difficult to accept for all but the most open-minded of organized market participants. This is because a plethora of incorrect knowledge that has been disseminated must be unlearned.

Knowledge provided in this book refutes the idea that markets move randomly and therefore cannot be understood. It refutes the idea that predicting market direction — a happenstance approach which indirectly relies on the strength of the individual — is a reliable way to approach a market. It refutes the efficient market theory belief that the market is "unbeatable," since all opportunities are equal because price and value are always identical in an organized market. It debunks some myths regarding risk. Lastly, it refutes the current approaches to trading that differ from the sound approach of investing.

Most persons approaching organized markets enter clouded by these assumptions, and begin by being lost from the ground up, unable to observe reality with a blank slate. For example, few participants who gain market knowledge from the second source understand a market's purpose, while those who have gained market knowledge from experience immediately agree with the statement that a market's purpose, the reason it exists, is to facilitate trade. (This is a statement the reader of this book will soon grow weary of.) In facilitating trade, the most important function of the marketplace — a function that is key to understanding it — is to provide market-generated information.

Another aim of this book is to refute the idea that knowledge of the marketplace must be bought. We hope to decentralize the ability to understand and profit from markets by showing that everyone has the ability to observe, reflect, analyze and make his own decisions in all market situations. We further hope that the reader sees the similarities of all things and concludes that in broad terms, most things financial are the same. The reader's challenge in understanding organized markets is to think and consider all possibilities which occur from a logical standpoint, to set aside current approaches to markets and learn to read them, monitoring them forward through time.

We hope to demystify the ability to understand an organized market. To understand a market is nothing more than reading market-generated information. Market-generated information has been in existence since the first marketplace and has been available to anyone who cares to seek or read it. It is the traditional financial world's lost resource. While market-generated information goes predominantly undiscovered or unnoticed in the organized markets, it nevertheless is of inestimable value to those few participants who understand the logic behind markets, and know how to find, read and interpret — and finally know how to act on it. The assumption behind relying on market-generated information — commonly done by a few very successful participants who are regularly close to a market — is that knowledge and understanding of the present is the key that unlocks the mystery of the market. It has import far beyond a standard high, low and close or the price of the most recent transaction.

Market-generated information differs markedly from outside information, information generated from a related source which can then be applied to the marketplace (e.g., the type of information Graham and Dodd studied: balance sheets, industry growth, demand or harvest projections, new management, etc.). Thus, market-generated information is not once removed, it is reality, and will only change through time. Therefore, it is not a potentially inaccurate prediction. (Consistently accurate predictions of future possibilities are not within the average person's capabilities, and poor predictions are often the antithesis of value.)

The key to understanding market-generated information lies in organizing the seemingly chaotic, seemingly random market activity into meaningful, measurable data segments which can be captured, defined and then monitored. This provides a sound basis for interpreting the price data and allows a person a sound decision-making process — to act or not to act. Thus, market-generated information is nothing more than a time-series plot of transactional data: price data plotted over time, formulated into a format which lends itself to statistical measurement and comparison. (In our case, we have chosen the bell curve, normal distribution. The following graphic, attributed to statistician W. J. Youden from *The Visual Display of Quantifiable Information,* says much about why the bell curve is significant to a market understanding.)

THE
NORMAL
LAW OF ERROR
STANDS OUT IN THE
EXPERIENCE OF MANKIND
AS ONE OF THE BROADEST
GENERALIZATIONS OF NATURAL
PHILOSOPHY* IT SERVES AS THE
GUIDING INSTRUMENT IN RESEARCHES
IN THE PHYSICAL AND SOCIAL SCIENCES AND
IN MEDICINE, AGRICULTURE AND ENGINEERING*
IT IS AN INDISPENSABLE TOOL FOR THE ANALYSIS AND THE
INTERPRETATION OF THE BASIC DATA OBTAINED BY OBSERVATION AND EXPERIMENT*

With the bell curve organizing data, reading and understanding market activity simply calls for being able to understand how, where, when and under what conditions participants use the market, then being able to isolate or key in on factors that are important at that time, while filtering out those factors which are unimportant. Reading the information generated from the marketplace *as it is generated* allows anyone to relate price against value, applying this knowledge of the present to his particular situation.

Beyond understanding the importance of knowledge of the present and the importance of arranging transactional data into the bell curve, the approach to markets advanced in this book incorporates two basic equations. The first is used to break down and define market reality. The equation is simply: **price + time = value.** This statement is known and even obvious to most intelligent persons; subconsciously we accept a known product's price as value as we repeatedly are charged that price over time. The equation also holds true for the most complex markets. It captures and defines a market's range of activity, creating a distinction between prices which are accepted as fair value and those prices which the market rejects as temporarily unfairly above or below value in the current timeframe.

The second equation is useful for defining a framework for accomplishing results. It shows that in a given market opportunity, **results = market understanding x (you + trading strategy).** This equation describes and pinpoints the areas which comprise successful trading or investing.

With all the market understanding this book will provide, the key to success still is the responsibility of the individual. Such an understanding will prevent an individual from placing himself in a position where he must function above reasonable expectations in order to succeed. He must have the ability to remain disciplined while integrating his thought process into his capabilities.

2

THE PRINCIPLES OF MARKET LOGIC, OPERATIONAL PROCEDURES AND CHARACTERISTICS

T he goal of the following section is to advance a rather straight-forward and logical argument: In order to understand a market's structure, one needs to read and gain an understanding of present market-generated information. Once this is accomplished, one is able to distinguish between types of market activity as well as prices. To provide the meat of the argument, the following principles have been stripped to their barest essentials and are presented in outline form. The principles presented in this outline, their implications for trading and investing implementation, and several definitions will be developed later in this section and illustrated in working examples in the second section.

Do not become intimidated by this outline. Skip it if you must, and refer back to it as you become comfortable with these concepts as they are developed and explained in later chapters.

I. A free marketplace is one in which participants are voluntarily active.

II. Required for a marketplace:
   A) product
   B) need for product

III. Purpose of the marketplace:
   A) to facilitate trade
      1) a location
      2) market-imposed timeframes

IV. Marketplace functions with:
   A) product
   B) need for product
   C) price promoting activity through excess
   D) time regulating activity

V. Marketplace advertises opportunity by offering price away from value.
   A) A response to this opportunity can be absent.
   B) A response can be present, taking advantage of the opportunity.
   C) A response can be opposite, overtaken by initiating activity
      unperceived by the marketplace at that moment.
      1) Activity is one which goes counter to the promotion for which
         the market is advertising.

VI. Marketplace is controlled and regulated through the distribution of
   price and time, yielding types of natural organization which produce
   balance (a "fair" area where two-sided trade takes place).

VII. The combination of all these components in an active phase is called
   market activity.
   A) Market activity is composed of a range of time-price opportunity
      occurrences, TPO being the market's basic unit of measurement.

VIII. Market activity is an expression of participant need, triggered by:
   A) market-imposed timeframes
   B) participant timeframes
      1) A market's volatility is dependent on the mix of long and short
         market-imposed and participant timeframes.

IX. Market activity generates information:
   A) A readable preference of variant time-price opportunities which
      occur at different times, at different or the same prices, at
      different or the same levels of volume. This is an expression of
      accepted, rejected or changing value by participants as a whole.
      1) Time-price opportunities (and hence prices) can appear with a
         large or small relative amount of time.
         a) Those time-price opportunities resulting in a large amount of
            time must result in large transactional volume and display
            market acceptance or value for both sides in that timeframe.
         b) Those time-price opportunities resulting in a small amount
            of time must result in small transactional volume and display
            market rejection or unfair value for one side in that
            timeframe.

B) This amounts to market distinction as to price.
   1) prices accepted versus prices rejected
C) A further distinction of the type of market activity can be made within the framework of acceptance/rejection.
   1) prices in a market-created opportunity which are responded to versus prices in a market-created opportunity which are overtaken by other initiating forces. Therefore,

    Price + Time = Market Acceptance (responsive or initiating)
             = Transactional Volume
             = Market Value (definition of all free markets)

X. All markets, although they may be structured differently (dealership, auction house, exchange market, etc.) are nevertheless motivated by the same forces, and operate based on these basic principles.
A) traders and investors should understand sound market logic so that they can extract and read market-generated information to satisfy their particular needs in every marketplace.

THE MARKET'S OPERATIONAL PROCEDURES

What the Market Does to Create Activity

A) The concerns and needs of the participants which collectively determine the activity of a marketplace are many and varied and can be different for different timeframes, but are brought to balance in the closest timeframe. These concerns and needs are not necessarily balanced in timeframes outside the closest parameter.
B) In balancing itself, the market focuses on a dominant set or single concern or news item -- whether real or imagined -- and neutralizes that in the very short run by offering a range of prices in order to locate an area which facilitates trade. In doing so, the market makes the situation fair to both sides in the closest timeframe.
C) Once balance is found, the marketplace will continue to trade in this fair area until another influence from either the immediate or longer term timeframe enters and upsets the balance, shifting to a new price area. This new balance can be changed by a new set of concerns or participants becoming active. This process can be continuous or opposite to the initial dominant concern in nature. In the short run, this process is rapid and volatile.
   1) Thus, the dominant concern usually motivates the short timeframe participants to change the price to create fairness.
   2) The dominant concern usually does not motivate the long timeframe participant. He is often motivated to take the "fair price area" as a market-created opportunity or price excess in his timeframe. In other words, the activity of the longer timeframe may upset the balance created in the short term.
D) The market provides a range of time-price opportunities on which participants can act. Their action or inaction determines the structure of the marketplace. The market rotates in order to bring in involvement of all timeframes and facilitate trade. The price area most accepted is the price area most often used, which therefore is the price area which facilitates trade, which is accepted as value.
E) The market will continuously offer various time-price opportunities to reassure this activity.
F) The nonaccepted prices are either over- or undercompensations used to find balance. It is these over- or undercompensations which motivate entrance by longer timeframe buying/selling participants, either desiring to take advantage of price away from

value or due to distress, and which are used as reference points for the short timeframe participant.

G) This over- or undercompensation is always present in the marketplace to a small or large extent, depending on volatility or commonplace among participants, which is dependent on the mix of timeframe influence.

H) The marketplace regulates itself and exercises control over its primary function, which is to facilitate trade. It does this when, as the market moves toward the extremes of the balance area, it becomes attractive for long timeframe participants, and at the same time attracts short timeframe traders. Thus, the market-created opportunity does not last long, because of increased competition to take advantage of the opportunity. This introduces time as the controlling factor in the marketplace.

Market Characteristics

I. All markets are essentially auction markets.
  A) There are two categories of auction markets.
    1) Active auction -- range develops during negotiation.
    2) Passive auction -- range is already predetermined in a packaged offering.
  B) Active auctions can go from low to high or from high to low. In the auction process, the market will continue in the same direction in an effort to facilitate trade until the last buyer or seller has participated.
  C) All prices change from the previous price for a purpose, that being to satisfy the condition of the market.

II. Participants have a spectrum of timeframe perspectives during which they operate. For simplicity, participants can be classified into two categories according to their timeframe perspective.
  A) Those conducting business for the short term (or day) -- short timeframes.
  B) Those conducting business outside this parameter - long (or other) timeframe.
    1) Those with different timeframes operate in the market differently.
      a) Short (day) timeframe - looking for fair price within a short time.
      b) Long (other) timeframe - looking for market-created opportunity where it relates to individual participant need, an elective type of activity.

III. Activity Levels for timeframes are as follows:
  A) Short timeframe participant activity usually makes up most of the transactional volume in a given timeframe.
  B) Long timeframe participant activity usually makes up a small amount of the volume in the same timeframe.
    1) Anxiety level for a short timeframe participant ranges from active to passive.
    2) Anxiety level for a long timeframe participant ranges from passive to active.
    3) Total mix of volume will be a blend of these circumstances and will affect the market's structure accordingly.

IV. Regardless of whether prices are in an excess, or are facilitating trade in the short timeframe, a market-created opportunity which is attractive to a long timeframe buyer will not be attractive to a

long timeframe seller. Thus, desire for participation for a
long-term buyer and a long-term seller are opposite at the same
price, at the same time. Therefore, long-term buyers almost never
buy from long-term sellers. Thus, no market exists which is composed
solely of long timeframe participants trading with one another.

V. Where prices are facilitating trade and are thus fair in the short
timeframe, a price or price area which is attractive for a short timeframe
buyer will be attractive to a short timeframe seller.

VI. The normal trading pattern has the short-term trader transacting
business with the long-term trader, yielding various buyer-seller
combinations: long timeframe versus short timeframe. Each
combination transacts business in varying quantities throughout the
structure of the range.

VII. Participants can and will change their timeframe depending upon the
situation as it relates to their needs. The effect of this is to
increase or decrease market activity.
  A) Long timeframe participants, when they decide to abandon their
     posture of only trading with an advantage and trade in the short
     timeframe, become short timeframe participants because their needs
     and goals as expressed in market activity become identical to
     those of other short timeframe participants. This increases
     market activity.
  B) Likewise, when long timeframe participants extend their timeframe,
     market activity is decreased. Further, when a long timeframe
     participant passes up a market-created opportunity, market
     activity decreases.
  C) When the short timeframe participant lengthens his timeframe, he
     becomes a long timeframe participant, decreasing activity.
  D) When the short timeframe participant shortens his timeframe,
     activity increases.
  E) Regardless of timeframe, those who have initiated positions in
     nonconsuming markets may look to exit the positions over either
     timeframe.

This concludes the presentation, in outline form, of the logic,
operational procedures and the characteristics involved and inherent in
all markets. While there are many diverse forms of markets, all adhere
to the logical principles as presented in this outline. The operational
procedures may not be explicit to the untrained eye in certain markets,
and minimum and maximum timeframes vary greatly depending on the
particular market. But nevertheless, every market is governed with the
logical and operational procedures and displays characteristics outlined
above. From these principles, one can develop and employ tools with
which to read and understand the market, providing the information
from which to act in a logical, well-thought-out and consistent manner.

3

SOME THOUGHTS ON THE RANDOM WALK AND EFFICIENT MARKET THEORIES

T here are a select few who regularly profit from their involvement in organized markets, and there is the great majority of people who do not. Among the points which distinguish successful traders and investors on one hand from the vast majority of market participants and most of the academic community on the other, are the acceptance by the latter group of the notion of organized markets as a random walk, and the ability to distinguish organized from unorganized markets because of the so-called "efficient market" theory.

The most important -- yet simplistic -- implication of market logic is that anyone can now locate value in an organized (or in fact any) market. Thus, one can determine when price is below value, at value or above it. Armed with this information, so long as one has the other requisite characteristics, one can join the ranks of the few who make money consistently in the organized markets. A secondary implication of market logic must therefore be that it refutes both the random walk and efficient market theories currently in vogue among the majority of the academic community. Consider each of these long-accepted theories regarding market activity.

Random Walk

The theory of price fluctuation as a random walk (and the term itself) has been used for centuries. There are numerous definitions of random walk, and each definition varies in shades depending on who is doing the defining. According to Robert Hagin's *Dow Jones-Irwin Guide to Modern Portfolio Theory,* random walk is a term used in mathematics and statistics to describe a process in which successive changes are statistically independent. A random walk implies (that the market's price displays) no discernible pattern of travel. The size and direction of the next step cannot be predicted from the size and direction of the last or even from all previous steps. The serial correlation is (functionally) zero. In other words, the random walk theory holds that it is impossible to predict tomorrow's price changes based on what has occurred today.

One of the central points developed throughout this book is that all markets operate similarly and are motivated by the same principles, and that anyone who can understand these principles — plus observe and record the individual characteristics of the specific market — and can employ a sound trading strategy and discipline himself, can profit handsomely from any market. Thus, a central thesis of market logic is that there is little distinction between organized or exchange-traded markets such as stocks, futures, options, etc., and all other so-called "unorganized" markets where no federally regulated exchange floor exists. (Certainly the exchange-traded markets often offer a narrower bid-ask spread, thus creating a higher degree of liquidity and hence lowering transaction costs as compared to those of unorganized markets.)

Every market is an auction market, either passive or active. In a passive auction, the individual does not take part in an active negotiating process but selects from products offered at different prices which make up the range. In an active auction, participants negotiate the range. Whether the auction is passive or active, all markets "auction" or trend up and down in order to fulfill their purpose, to facilitate trade. In an auction, prices do not develop randomly, but rather to fulfill the purpose of the auction.

The purpose of any market is to facilitate trade. Lack of trade facilitation inevitably causes price to move. This price movement behavior is as true in the organized markets as it is in a grocery store or any other everyday market. Thus, price changes to satisfy the condition of the market and every price is a result of the condition of the market. The fact that price moves for a specific reason further precludes price from developing in a random manner.

Furthermore, prices are not statistically independent of each other. Price, in moving to satisfy the condition of the market, provides an informational flow. In other words, markets must generate trade, and in doing so, prices fluctuate, generating information about where trade is being conducted and where it is not. This information is valuable to the market participant, as we shall soon demonstrate. [1] But true randomness does not generate valuable information. In other words, in statistically random situations, knowledge of the present is not important, for it conveys no advantage. If knowledge of the present structure of a market is important and does convey an advantage — as we shall see in later chapters — a market cannot be a random walk.

We shall see how, in a futures market, the day's activity is structured; price moves because of the degree of each timeframe's participation at various levels of price. We shall see why the ultimate structure of a futures market for one day depends on the activity level of the various groups. We shall see that the market develops logically, as price fulfills the need of the market. And, we shall see that prices can be distinguished from one another yielding valuable information.

Efficient Markets

According to Robert Hagin, *The efficient market theory is the assertion that in a market with numerous investors who prefer high returns over low returns and low risk over high risk, "information" is of no value. An investor can attain no more nor less than a fair return for the risks undertaken.*

In the semi-strong form, the efficient market theory hypothesizes a market in which all publicly available information is efficiently impounded on the price of a stock, and hence a market in or item of publicly available information that can be used to predict future price changes.

An efficient market does not allow price to get away from value, since the theory holds that information is of no value since it is factored into the market, as every price must represent fair value. If price is always in equilibrium of value, then the theory presumes that prices are indistinguishable from one another in all but number. Thus, according to the efficient market hypothesis, all prices represent value, and the market is balanced at every moment; all the needs and concerns of the entire marketplace -- participants in every known and unknown timeframe -- are brought to the present by a price representing value for all. This seldom occurs and when it does, it is happenstance, and nondiscernible except by the lack of activity.

Different participants have different timeframes for buying and/or selling; longer timeframe participants seek to buy low and sell high, and short timeframe participants must transact sooner and cannot be as discriminating. Thus, all markets — including organized markets — are inefficient from the standpoint that participants with differing timeframes view the most recent price with differing opinions and do not participate at the same time and at the same price. In other words, a given price is not viewed as an equal opportunity for all. The market cannot at any one moment balance all the needs and concerns of the entire marketplace — participants in every known and unknown timeframe — since the most recent price does not represent the same thing to all participants. In other words, no single price represents fair value for everyone. [2]

Rather than being efficient, all organized markets are effective. They are effective from the standpoint that they produce and regulate trade, bringing into play all participants over time. In other words, the market facilitates trade from all participants, not with each individual price, but over a large sample size. The fact that participants with different timeframes exist precludes a price dominated by one time-frame from being fair value for all. The efficient market hypothesis overlooks the existence of participant timeframes.

The assumption of randomness and the "efficient market hypothesis" assumes that the market -- price movement over time -- conveys no knowledge or information. Instead, it assumes that if a trader profits from a market, he has resorted to predicting, and his luck will sooner or later run out. However, one need not predict the future in a market of uncertainty. It is impossible to always accurately predict future events. But we can monitor the market, understand its present condition, and how current price relates to the market's current assessed value, and from this, we can logically deduce probable behavior, and adjust our assessment from the new information the market provides as it unfolds. And by extracting bits of market-generated information, we can deduce and change.

The Academic Community's Ball and Chain

One rule that most successful individuals and businesses have incorporated into their operating procedure is not to pursue any endeavor in which they face a disadvantage before correcting those things that create their disadvantage. In other words, it is important to continually assess and reassess what is producing successful results, discarding what does not yield success.

Yet, the academic community continues to pursue the refinement of studies based on fallacious assumptions about the market, particularly the random walk and efficient market theories. Gaining knowledge from experience has not been practiced by the academic community, not out of malfeasance, but because in modern society knowledge can more easily be gained from a formal classroom teaching environment. Instead of examining reality, rethinking fundamental market assumptions, and seeking a new course of thought such as is introduced in this book, the academic community continues to pursue the disadvantage as taught in the classroom.

This is not meant to be a pedantic indictment of the academic mindset. Clearly, it is difficult in most institutions to gain a true evaluation of reality. It is even more difficult within an institutional setting for the status quo to change, regardless of whether what is accepted is correct or not. The academic community is not guilty of anything worse than not taking a leadership role in thinking logically about markets. But times have changed.

---

[1] Those who understand the condition of the market (where price over time is building value) are conveyed an advantage from which they can profit whereas those who focus on prices against each other must assume randomness and no understanding. (This will be explained and developed in the ensuing chapters.)

[2] In order to understand the market's inefficiency, consider the reality of how markets function. A normal preoccupation of the short timeframe participant is to focus on the dominant concern or news focus. The dominant concern causes the market to be balanced in the eyes of the shortest timeframe participants. It is the short timeframe participants who normally transact the vast quantity of total volume. But while the short timeframe participants transact up to 90% of the volume, their presence does not change the market. Thus, this dominant concern may or may not be a dominant concern for the longer timeframe participants, since it may or may not be of major significance to the supply and demand situation in the framework of the total marketplace. It is the focusing of the short timeframe participants on a relatively unimportant piece of news, a dominant concern that is not of major significance, that causes price excess. In other words, a minor piece of news -- a fact or perception that might be only 2% of the total timeframe decisions of the marketplace -- will motivate 80-90% of the day's or week's trade, since the short timeframe participants, who are the majority of the market, focus on it. Their preoccupation can create an opportunity when it is considered an excess for the longer timeframe participants. This leads one to wonder, how can all prices be equal, and how can all prices represent value when short timeframe over-compensation presents an opportunity for a more realistic valuation in a larger timeframe? (These terms and concepts will be explained and developed in the ensuing chapters.)

4

COMPONENTS OF A
MARKETPLACE

REFLECTIONS ON THE FIRST TWO
BASIC OBSERVATIONS

T he principles outlined in the second chapter and the form in which they have been presented are admittedly difficult to grasp at first blush. Anyone who might be intimidated by their placement should have skipped over them during his first reading. To help explain and aid in an understanding of these concepts, the following three chapters will illustrate the principles espoused in the outline by taking a step back from the theoretical and presenting concrete reality. Once the reader feels comfortable with each principle, it is recommended that the Chapter 2 outline be read and reread until it is fully understood and no longer intimidating.

The goal of this chapter will be to provide a primitive and introductory examination of markets. This should begin to clear up several misconceptions about the function of markets which have caused great confusion. By illustrating several market principles in a simple and easily comprehended situation, each reader's basic understanding of markets should be reinforced. The following will point out that while all the details of market principles may not be fully understood yet, each consumer does in fact already have a subconscious market understanding, which allows him to fulfill his everyday needs. It is this unconscious understanding which is each individual's foundation for building a more complete knowledge of any market.

Price and Value

Most investors and traders distinguish between understandable market situations where price and value differ, and the organized markets, where price and value are always the same. Unknown to most participants, all markets — not just the unorganized, everyday markets -- have a universal commonality: price and value differ in all markets, and the underlying principles which motivate buying and selling are identical. (Most investors and traders in organized markets inherently understand this, but it was most notably presented in Graham and Dodd's *Securities Analysis.*) Further, every market reflects the collective needs and goals of its participants through its range of activity. In order to understand any marketplace, one needs to separate and isolate that part of the range which motivated the activity of each category of participant.

But while most market examinations begin by focusing on the participants, a true understanding of market logic necessitates taking a step back and examining and understanding the real purpose of a market, and the importance which knowledge of this purpose has in all market understanding. Understanding the purpose of the marketplace is the key to being able to benefit from it. However, it is very easy to be misled and confuse the outward results of the marketplace -- that price is rationing supply and demand — with its purpose, the reason it exists.

The Purpose of a Market

A marketplace exists solely to facilitate trade. This is its only purpose. And this fact is the starting point and a key concept to grasp when analyzing or participating in any marketplace.

As mentioned above, to understand any marketplace one also must grasp the needs and goals which motivate its participants. In a marketplace, the needs and goals which motivate participants are expressed in their continued buying and/or selling. Thus, observing and reflecting on the inherent needs and goals of a participant aids in gaining a market understanding, but observing his market participation — his buying and selling agenda in the marketplace — provides valuable information, which is the foundation for an accurate market understanding and for buy-sell decision making.

Comprehending why it is true that markets exist solely to facilitate trade, and the remaining logical principles and considerations behind every market, is made easier by considering the situation of a single producer and a single consumer who transact trade prior to the existence of a centralized marketplace, then as a marketplace is developing, and once again as part of a large and complex marketplace.

Prior to a Marketplace

Where no centralized marketplace exists, so long as there is a product and a need for a product, there will of course be trade. In other words, a single producer and a single consumer can transact business. In doing so, they make a market, but not a true marketplace. Without a marketplace, a very provincial and inflexible situation exists for both sides of the transaction, namely the buyer (consumer) and seller (producer). Only a limited flow of information is available. Furthermore, that information is not circulating to either producer or consumer in an effective manner.

This situation leaves the consumer less informed as to the costs and benefits of the product – how much it should cost and how it may satisfy his need, etc. Therefore, he is in a weak position to fulfill his primary goal: to buy enough of the product to satisfy his need as inexpensively as possible. To fulfill his goal, he needs to evaluate the product in terms of its usefulness, consider what possible substitutes exist and weigh any other information vital to determining value.

While every consumer has a different need, every producer has the same need: to stay in business by selling his product. Since a producer's primary goal is to maximize profits, he is always seeking to determine the price where his profits are maximized and adjust likewise. For instance, he would gladly produce more at a lower price if, in doing so, he could sell more and receive per-unit savings through economies of scale, passing on only a percentage of these savings to the consumers. In doing so, he would fulfill his goal of maximizing profits.

But where no marketplace exists, the producer does not gain needed information from a transaction. He would like to know how the product meets the consumer's individual needs over a range of prices. In other words, is he selling the product at, above or below value for the majority of potential customers? Without a location where his product can be compared with others, the producer cannot better his marketing situation by improving or repricing the product, because he doesn't have enough information about how the product could be selling in a competitive situation.

Furthermore, without a marketplace, there is no timeframe during which the consumer can indicate whether he wants more or less of the product at a given price. In short, there is no efficient way for the producer to increase his business -- to facilitate trade -- without a marketplace.

Even a contract between a buyer and seller to transfer goods for a fixed price at regular intervals does not facilitate trade or information in the way that a marketplace situation does. While the contract may be beneficial to the interests of both parties when they enter it, there is no flexibility and no way to expand trade other than by communicating with each other. A contract aids the situation, but it does not facilitate increased trade, only the amount that is warranted at the time the contract is negotiated.

Coming back to our situation, both the producer and the consumer wish to improve their lot, since they are fundamentally self-interested individuals who want to satisfy their needs and fulfill their goals. Indeed, one cannot easily find an example of a product manufacturer or distributor in any free economy who does not wish to do more business — to facilitate more trade.

Unable to improve their lot, both parties are frustrated without a marketplace. They need a more effective communication and distribution system in order to satisfy their particular needs and goals. They need an arrangement or entity which will facilitate trade.

Developing a Marketplace

Both the producer and consumer realized that a lot more of the goods and services could be sold if potential customers were aware that goods were regularly for sale at a certain time at a certain place. This would benefit the producer by fulfilling both his need to stay in business and his goal to maximize profits. At the same time, the consumer would be able to satisfy his personal need and would be in a stronger position to meet his goal of fulfilling his need as cheaply as possible.

At some point the two arrange to meet regularly at fixed time intervals in order to determine if an exchange of the producer's product for the consumer's currency can take place. A marketplace is born. With such a meeting agreement, increased communication and product distribution can now take place. As a springboard for fulfilling both parties' needs and goals by facilitating trade, the marketplace soon becomes a reliable institution. More goods can be examined, compared and ultimately purchased by the consumer, while more goods can be produced, competitively priced to maximize profits, and ultimately sold by the producer. Both consumer and producer are provided a range of opportunities to act or not act upon, a situation where competition dictates value.

A marketplace provides the ability for both parties to any transaction to satisfy their need and maximize their goals at the practical level of reality through increased trade and competition. Thus, a marketplace always serves both the producer's and consumer's needs, and is by definition required to do so if it is to flourish. Indeed, without the need to facilitate trade on both sides of the producer-consumer equation, no marketplace can survive for long. In other words, transactional volume in a marketplace will dry up when that marketplace does not meet the needs of both producer and consumer while allowing every participant to maximize his goals.

A marketplace has a centralized location, regular hours, dependable participants and, most importantly, it fosters competition among both producer and consumer and is therefore expandable.

A Mature Market

The mature marketplace may take the form of a franchise, a distributorship, a series of franchises or distributorships, a jobber network or one or a series of wholesale or retail outlets, or, of course, an organized exchange where stocks, futures, and/or options are traded. Regardless, a mature marketplace continually seeks to facilitate trade, thereby allowing producers to maximize profits and consumers to fulfill needs. A mature marketplace expands the distribution of goods, allowing more business to be transacted. Both producer and consumer know they can conduct a varied quantity of business at a mature marketplace, should they choose to, given prevailing prices. Thus, the form or structure of a marketplace is not important, so long as the mature marketplace meets the location, time, participant, and most importantly, the competition requirements. If it does, both parties benefit from the marketplace's existence, since they can use the information it generates to facilitate more trade.

The most valuable service any marketplace provides involves generating and disseminating information. That the marketplace is an informational source is illustrated by considering any and every type of marketplace, but especially an auction house. For instance, the noted aution houses Christie's and Sotheby's market art, antiques, collectibles, and any other objects in limited supply. The format for marketing, the auction, is a type of marketplace. The purpose which causes clients to come to these house auctions is the same as in every market, not to ration supply and demand, but to facilitate trade in the market -- the art, antique and collectibles market.

The first step toward conducting a successful auction of this type includes advertising and promoting the products to be auctioned to the target market, the art, antique or collectibles world. The art world recognizes the value of information on past art transactions for similar products, and weighs it in deciding reasonable expectations for future value. Thus, past auction results — transactional information — are researched avidly by all participants prior to the next auction. The transactional information provided by an open auction market serves as valuable information for both potential and actual buyers and sellers.

After the fact, the auction results are published and distributed. The transactional data reflect the condition of the market while serving as an advertisement to facilitate more trade, possibly bringing more works of art out into the market for sale or attracting more collectors as buyers. Those wishing to assess the market for their personal collection now realize that its value has gone up or down or stayed the same, depending, of course, on the prices comparable works fetched. Again, there is a desire on the part of the auction house and the art community to transact more business. They are enabled to do this because they have inherent marketplaces.

Conclusion

The major goal of this primitive and introductory examination of markets was to clear up several misconceptions about the function of markets which have caused confusion. Two very significant points have been clearly illustrated: whether it is an organized, federally regulated financial exchange, an open air food mart, or anything in between, the sole reason any marketplace exists is not to ration supply and demand, nor to allocate scarce resources, but simply to facilitate trade. Furthermore, all functioning markets generate information while advertising opportunity. Any logical understanding of any market must begin by acknowledging these fundamental principles of every market-place.

5

COMPONENTS OF A MARKETPLACE

RELECTIONS ON THE THIRD AND FOURTH BASIC OBSERVATIONS

T he goal of this chapter will be to provide an understanding of the components the marketplace uses to facilitate trade, advertise opportunity, and generate information.

Every marketplace functions with four components: the product and the interests of the producer-participant, the need on the part of the consumer-participant, price, and time.

The Product and the Interests of the Producer-Participant

The product must satisfy a need, or else be packaged or marketed in such a way as to persuade the participants that it satisfies a need. The producer is a self-interested individual whose need is to remain in business and whose goal is to maximize profits. He wishes to facilitate trade in his product in order to determine the price at which profits are maximized.

The Need on the Part of the Consumer-Participant

Consumer-participants have their own individual purpose for using the market. These purposes are many and varied and in all but the most organized markets, they reflect the consumer's need for the product. The participant's goal is to fulfill his need as cost-effectively as possible and to determine the quantity of purchase needed to do so. Every product has a value in the mind of each consumer. In establishing the product's value, each consumer weighs the product's costs and benefits through time.

Price

Price, the market component most participants rely on when making trading decisions, is the amount of money given or set as consideration for the sale of a specified item. It is a variable and, as such, it fluctuates. Price facilitates trade by balancing the market, making the situation fair for both producer and consumer over the very short run.

The market, in facilitating trade, uses price to promote activity. Price does this by advertising opportunity, moving up or down in order to make the market attractive for participants to enter. The market continually uses the shifting or vacillation of price between the area where it encourages buying (consuming) and where it encourages selling (producing).

Price, endlessly promoting activity through advertising opportunity in the market in an effort to facilitate trade, does so by testing excess levels. However, the market has little or no trade activity when price moves either to too high or too low an excess. Thus, when price moves either too low or too high, it does not facilitate trade and must eventually change.

To prevent price from moving too extensively in one direction, the marketplace has "hidden brakes," namely the self-interest of the participants. If price becomes unfairly above or below value, one of the parties to the producer-consumer equation will not trade or will trade in decreasing volume. For example, as price moves up, it advertises opportunity to producers, but may be in an area where the consumers will not buy, or will buy grudgingly and in smaller volume, thus forcing the producers to lower price over time.

The promotional ability of excess price and the hidden brakes inherent in every marketplace can be illustrated by a business custom existing in most Western cultures, the "post-holiday sale." During this period, most department stores substantially discount merchandise not sold at regular prices during the holiday season, which for the retailer is the period of greatest inventory demand, due to a great supply of buyers. Store management realizes that after the holiday season a shortage of buyers exists, and merchandise not sold at regular pre-holiday prices will not move quickly. The retailer's primary goal throughout the year is to be quickly rid of slow-moving inventory which is costing interest, storage and insurance while always increasing liquidity. Hence, merchandise is repriced downward. Furthermore, merchandise will be sold only if repriced at enough of a discount to attract so-called bargain hunters.[3] Thus, every post-holiday sale is a market's use of a "purpose (low excess) price" designed to move old inventory not sold during the holiday season. The retailer is willing to promote his leftover inventory through an excess low price, since only the excess price reduction will accomplish the goal.

As for this market's hidden brakes: Shoppers perceive these new lower prices as bargains because for the months leading into the holidays, these same items cost much more. For example, a shirt which had sold for $50 for the previous nine months, offered after the holidays for $25, gets participants to react. They realize they're buying price below the value established over the prior months. (Thus, shoppers have an association of price over time equaling value, not as an acknowledged and articulated principle, but rather as a perceived, almost unconscious insight.) The hidden brake which prevents the shirt from selling for $10 is the self-interest of the retailer, who assumes that 50% off will be as much of a price excess as he needs to fulfill his goal in the time allocated.

Thus, while low price excess attracts consumers, high price excess attracts producers. Another example of price excess promoting activity -- this time a high excess and hence promoting activity among producers -- can be seen in land values and prices hotels can charge when a new demand for hotel rooms is created. The management of seasonal motels located in resort areas expects strong demand which allows charging the highest prices only during the seasonal periods. Illustrated in chart form (the price charged per room against time), these seasonal periods represent the market high and a brief time relationship as well, while the remainder of the year, the "off season," represents the lower average price.

Suppose that a major amusement theme park opens some miles away, creating vast demand for nearby hotel space. A lone hotel next to the park is now able to charge twice what the above motels charge during the off-season, yet still remains fully booked. This high or excess price charged by the lone hotel is providing information to competitors. This information will inevitably promote activity in land values around the resort park, since vendors of resort-related services envision substantial profits, profits the lone hotel is making. Thus, high prices attract more (producers) sellers, who buy up land (at higher values) and build hotels. The so-called hidden brakes, the self-interest of the hotel guests, are such that as increased hotel space becomes available, assuming a fixed demand, prices will fall and the excess price charged by the lone hotel will soon be lowered to maximize profitability.

Thus, one of the most important insights that the information provided by a marketplace will provide to both producer and consumer is that activity is being shut off at a certain price. This is a signal that price is not facilitating trade or promoting activity and that this level should be offered only for a short period of time and thus is an excess and can be expected to move. For example, when a new, higher price produces a substantially lower level of activity, it signals to the producer that, for the moment, a lower price (or a corrective marketing strategy such as advertising, etc.) is needed if sales of the product or service are to pick up.

Similarly, if the producer, for whatever reason, lowers the price beyond the point where he can make an equitable profit, he will soon shut off the availability of the product at the unreasonably low price and will raise the price.

Time

Time, the market component few participants rely on when making trading decisions, illustrates the degree of change between need and price in the marketplace. It is a known constant, a measurement which participants inadvertently use when determining value through transactional data. Time impacts trade by regulating the duration during which buying (consuming) and selling (producing) can take place.

The market, in facilitating trade, uses price to promote opportunity and uses time to regulate it. In other words, the market uses time to regulate how long a given opportunity will be available, insuring that when price promotes opportunity to the point of reaching excess, that price is held in check. The market continually uses time to regulate itself throughout its structure. In other words, time at a given price yields volume, which the market equates with value. Everything else being equal, the more time at a price or price area, the more transactional volume, and the more value.

Examples of how time regulates price activity are illustrated in both the examples previously used to illustrate how price promotes activity. In the post-holiday sale, while the department store management was willing to sell at prices half of those charged prior to the holidays, management was not willing to offer this "below value" opportunity for long, but only until the current inventory is sold. Had the store extended the opportunity to purchase merchandise into what is considered the regular shopping season, the lower post-holiday sale prices would soon be considered the new value area. This is something no retailer would want to see. Retail stores and other producers/sellers use the lower excess price to promote activity only so long as it fulfills the purpose behind the excess price. Interestingly, the sharper the price reduction -- or the farther the price offered is below value -- the shorter the time period during which the opportunity will be available.

Likewise, the example of the resort hotel illustrates that time regulates activity. In that example, higher price promoted activity among producers, thereby attracting new hotels. The high prices charged first by the lone hotel and then by the new hotel market entrants were in hindsight an excess which occurred only until the demand for hotel space was met and exceeded. This activity (rising land values and hotel construction) continued until it went too high (hotels saturate the demand) and activity at the high prices was shut off. Thus, while the hotel near the resort park could temporarily charge prices considered above value, the market's excess promoted this opportunity to others, so that the hotel was not able to sustain the high prices and low vacancy status for long. Thus, through a long time-frame, time regulates the high price activity and controls it.

Both consumer and producer are interested in generating the maximum amount of activity at the most advantageous price possible. Thus, in reaching a balance, the market will produce extremes in the marketplace that will not hold over time, since they will be attractive for one side, but not attractive for the other. In order to balance, the market needs to go too high and too low to find an area that is fair for both parties over a period of time. It is these excesses on both sides that give the market its natural organization and provide information to participants.

When changes in price occur that are so small and subtle that activity is not shut off, there is no excess in the marketplace, and the market is in position to trend or show slow and consistant continuation. Thus, from a relative standpoint the market is either going to be working with excess or operating with slight, subtle changes.

Conclusion

The components which combine to make up a marketplace interact as follows: the marketplace controls and regulates itself through its allocation of price and time, yielding types of natural organization which, in producing excesses to test market acceptance, produce balance and provide information.

The obvious conclusion is a major breakthrough for anyone who understands market logic. The conclusion flies in the face of the conventional wisdom which says that price is the only mechanism that the market uses to balance or ration supply and demand. (Introductory economic theory asserts this, econometric models are built assuming it, and many investors and traders have experienced setbacks believing it.) However, when participants focus on price and price alone, they simply cannot have a market understanding. Thus, an analysis of a price versus price is inherently narrowly focused and virtually meaningless.

---

[3] It is important to recognize that the retailer's action in offering lower prices brings about two events. First, a percentage of the short timeframe shoppers may extend their timeframe and buy more than the usual quantity of shirts. Secondly, those long timeframe shoppers who were uninterested in buying a shirt at the normal price become motivated to buy at the lower bargain price.

6

COMPONENTS OF A MARKETPLACE

REFLECTIONS ON THE BEHAVIORAL OBSERVATIONS

The combination of a product plus self-interested individuals with a need for the product, plus price and time, combine to yield market activity, which represents the collective activity of all market participants. Market activity is organized into a range of time-price opportunities. In other words, a marketplace does not offer a price, but a range of prices from which the market participants can choose.

Time-price opportunities are the basic units of measurement which make up and define market activity, displaying any and all changes in the marketplace. Just as molecular activity is made up of atoms, so is market activity made up of time-price opportunities. However, these opportunities are undefined constant units of measurement which every market participant may define differently for each market.

A time-price opportunity is a point in time during which anyone may act as either a buyer or seller at a specific price. Again, there is nothing mysterious about such opportunities; they result naturally from price promoting activity and time regulating activity. They are significant to an understanding of a market because they allow the participant who examines this variable against a constant to go beyond the seeming randomness and unlock the natural organization of the market.

Timeframes

All market activity is triggered by two considerations, market-imposed timeframes and participant timeframes. Both market-imposed and participant (or individual) timeframes are forcing points in time which force or bring to the fore market activity by participants. All trading decisions are influenced by both types of timeframe considerations. Thus, timeframes collectively determine time-price opportunities in every market. Every marketplace has to service the timeframe needs or perspectives of every participant, producer and consumer alike, which, as previously mentioned above, it does through participation.

One example of a market-imposed timeframe -- and therefore a known constant and inflexible point which forces decision-making -- is the hours during which the marketplace operates. A sense of organization and dependability comes from regular marketplace hours, that time period during which trade can be transacted. Participants must tailor their decision-making around this time period. For example, people often find themselves acting differently near closing time from the way they act when that particular forcing point is not of dominant concern. Other examples of market-imposed timeframes include the date of the next Treasury auction, the anticipated timeframe for a new tax measure, tomorrow's weather, government estimates of the new crop harvest, or the next model year's car.

Market-imposed timeframes -- whatever they may be -- force both producer and consumer into having participant or individual time-frames -- points of forced decision-making. Thus, all participants in a market have independent timeframe considerations which are not a known constant, but are flexible and will change as advantageous opportunities are created and/or the individual's needs change. Each participant's independent timeframe is established by weighing his perceptions of particular short- and long-term need for the product, plus his individual time horizon, against his expectations of the future availability or supply of the product at the current cost, plus his current and future ability to pay.

A good example of a market-imposed timeframe, a participant timeframe, and how the former influences the latter can be seen in the setting of an auction market alluded to earlier. When Sotheby's or Christie's auctions off a particular object that is in limited supply, the market-imposed timeframe for that item will be the auctioneer's call, "going once...going twice..." followed by the rap of the gavel. This is a known and constant signal to participants, a market-imposed timeframe which forces every potential buyer's need or desire at the current price to the surface, with the outcome being an individual decision made by every participant on whether or not to raise the bid. An auction's market-imposed timeframe influences the participant timeframe in that one either buys during that timeframe or misses the opportunity. This illustrates how market activity can change by the market timeframe overriding the individual timeframe or the individual timeframe overriding the market-imposed timeframe. There is more activity in the first, and less activity in the second.

Timeframes, whether market-imposed or participant, are forward in nature, and range from the very short-term to the very long-term. An illustration of a relatively short timeframe market occurrence is the post-holiday sale alluded to previously. The sale comes and goes within the span of a few weeks, and is thus but a small percentage of the market's yearly activity. In contrast, an illustration of a relatively long timeframe market occurrence might be the lone resort hotel which was able to charge a sustained above-value price due to the increased demand brought on by the new theme park. Participants with short timeframe perspectives differ from those with long timeframes, both in obvious ways and in some ways not so obvious. The most obvious distinction involves how each views time. Short timeframe participants deal only with the immediate future and the nearby, not focusing on the longer view. If a participant must buy a new suit today, he must by necessity have a short timeframe. Thus, he will compare value among those stores he can see today, but he cannot wait until the next clearance sale before purchasing. In other words, he cannot consider if he is purchasing below value in the longer timeframe of the next six months, but must consider where the best value is among the suits available today. He is looking for a fair price in today's timeframe.

In contrast, longer timeframes and participants with longer timeframe perspectives tend to disregard the importance of the immediate future, but instead try to place short timeframe market activity within the context of the longer timeframe activity. For example, the individual who needs a suit in six months must buy a suit, but can do so at any time within the next six months. He views the suit market from a long timeframe. He will only enter the market when he finds a suit attractively priced, meaning today's price is sufficiently below the average price or value in the long timeframe. In other words, he is relating the short timeframe market opportunity -- it may be a "Spring Clearance" -- to his timeframe. In such a way, he judges that by taking advantage of the retailer's short timeframe need -- to quickly move suits not sold at higher prices -- he can buy below what is value over the larger timeframe. He is looking for an advantageous price.

Aside from the difference between how they view time, or how much importance they attach to recent market activity, participants from different timeframes differ in that they focus on different concerns and buy or sell for different reasons. Short timeframe participants buy or sell because they need to; long timeframe participants buy or sell not because they need to, but because they can take advantage of price away from value.

It is significant to note that long timeframe participants conduct transactions with those with shorter timeframes, not other long timeframe participants. In other words, a long timeframe buyer is trying to purchase used cars at a price below value. A long timeframe used car seller -- one who is under no pressure to sell -- wishes only to sell at a price at or (more probably) above value. The price at which the long timeframe buyer wishes to purchase is not a price acceptable to the long timeframe seller at the same time, and vice versa.

Timeframes determine when and at what price participants buy and sell. And participants with short timeframe perspectives differ in their buy-sell patterns from participants with long timeframe perspectives. These two concepts are keys to understanding market logic. They should be reviewed again and again until they are completely clear.

The Importance of Timeframes

Understanding the concepts of timeframes and their influence on the market is key because acknowledging them is necessary to be able to grasp the next concept: to the extent that one can isolate or separate out and read the activity of the various timeframe influences, one can gauge the strength or weakness of a market. In other words, in order to understand the market, one should endeavor to understand the current actions of the long versus short timeframe participants. This is why participants should be isolated and categorized by the length of their individual timeframe, their ability to remain patient in buying or selling, in order for one to gain a market understanding. For example, one should find out whether the long timeframers are predominantly buying aggressively from the short timeframers, whether they are liquidating, etc.

At any one time, any timeframe can be exerting the force that controls the market. However, the greatest amount of activity in every market comes from participants with the shortest timeframes. In other words, participants with short timeframes dominate normal market activity, mostly because they must commit to a position in the market much more than participants with a long timeframe. Short timeframe participants do not have the luxury to wait for a price away from value, they must wait merely for a fair price. Furthermore, participants with longer timeframes tend not to overcommit to the marketplace and therefore do not play a dominant role in day-to-day market activity except at price excesses.

In any futures market, for example, by far the greatest majority of the trades transacted on a normal day (in the area of 80%) are for immediate or short timeframe needs. The balance are those trans-actions of the longer timeframe, and are intended to be held until the next day, the next week, or the next year. The same is true of all other marketplaces. On any given day in the supermarket, for example, perhaps only 15% of purchasing is done by the long timeframe participants -- those fulfilling their shopping needs for some item they do not need during the next few weeks or months. The vast majority of purchasing is done by the short timeframe participants — those shopping for their needs for the day, week or near term.

However, when price falls to levels attractive to long timeframe participants, the ratio of near-term to long-term timeframe activity shifts, and with it, so will volume and ultimately price.

To oversimplify somewhat, consider the distinction between the two situations:

SITUATION 1

Short timeframe participants dominate market activity.

WHY: Long timeframe participants are absent because price and value are near to one another in long timeframes.

SITUATION 2

Long timeframe participants in conjunction with short time-frame participants dominate market activity.

WHY: Both are present because short timeframe participants always exist and long timeframe participants (either true long timeframe participants or short timeframe participants who have converted due to the opportunity) are attracted because of a market-created opportunity — price is away from value over a long timeframe.

Situation 1 is illustrated in the suit buying example, where the long timeframe participant has sufficient time in which to operate; he will not make buy or sell decisions motivated by anything other than value. Because he has sufficient time in which to operate, he will most likely buy only when he can take advantage of excess price caused by another participant focusing on maximizing his goals in the short timeframe. (When the long timeframe trader passes up opportunities, he loses time and thereby shortens his timeframe perspective.) Situation 2 is illus-trated in the discussion of the fact that lower prices offered in the price excess known as "Spring Clearance" motivated buying on the part of the long timeframe participant. Thus, the reason clearance sales do not continue for a substantial portion of time and yet generate a substantial portion of the total transaction volume is that both short and long timeframe participants are actively buying.

Thus, when long timeframe participants buy, the market is either perceived by them to be undervalued or they are forced to take advantage because they believe they are missing the opportunity. And, as we have also seen from that example, individuals with the shortest timeframes do not have as many options open, nor do they have as much time in which to think and act. Often they are forced to buy or sell regardless of the relationship of price to value over a long timeframe. An example of this in an organized marketplace might be the individual forced to liquidate a market position by a certain time or day due to an inability to meet margin requirements.

Thus, changing the mix of timeframe participants is the only factor that changes the condition of the market, increasing transactional volume and ultimately moving price. Another example might be the supermarket which promotes activity in a nonperishable item through a sale. The transactional volume of the reduced item is increased, since long timeframe shoppers are added to the normal number of short timeframe shoppers (and many short timeframe shoppers extend their timeframe, buying more than their normal quantity to build an inventory of the item), since it is priced below value. Price must now shift upward, because the grocer is selling an increasing amount of the item at near or below a break even price. The increased transactional volume necessitates his ultimately increasing the price to balance the market.

The greatest percentage of activity in a market exists to satisfy the near term -- the hand to mouth needs of the short timeframe participants -- while the long timeframe activity dominates the marketplace only occasionally. Yet it is the entrance of the long timeframe participants that changes the condition of the market and causes range extension or price movement. It does so by upsetting the delicate balance that has been predominant. Further, it is price excesses created by the short timeframe participants which create opportunities for the longer time-frame participants. Thus, participants in various timeframes compete against each other, seeking to take advantage of one another. The long timeframe participant takes advantage of price away from value while the short timeframe participant exploits the complacency of the long timeframe, thereby forcing a change in his outlook.

Thus, in order to have a market understanding, one must examine what long timeframe participants are doing and how short timeframe participants are reacting. Hence, the challenge of understanding the market is to isolate, categorize and analyze the activity of the different timeframe participants.

How Changes in Price Affect Value's Movement

As we have seen, long-term market-imposed or participant timeframes have a great influence on day-to-day market activity only when price gets far enough away from value to make it attractive for long timeframe participants to buy price below value or sell price above value. Thus, it is price getting far enough away from value which attracts longer timeframe participation and in so doing, changes the condition of the market.

But what happens when price moves away from value, but not far enough to encourage long timeframe participants to enter and take advantage of the disparity between price and value in the shorter timeframe? Simply put, when this happens, the conditions of the market do not change, and the new price becomes accepted as the new fair value over time. In other words, when conditions do not change, the market is in a position to continue its behavior. Some markets tend to trend more than others because of the timeframe mix of the participants.

Contrasting the housing market with the oil market from the very longest timeframe illustrates this distinction. The U.S. housing market has been in a trending market, representing a continuously higher movement in value since the depression of the 1930s. Many areas have experienced cycles where neighborhood housing values appreciated as much as 5% a year continuously for a decade. Why?

When the velocity or increment of price change is such that it does not change the behavior of market participants, the market is set to trend. In other words, the higher prices did not motivate enough long timeframe homeowners to sell. Thus, the housing market has been able to continue in a strong bull market only because price didn't move far enough from value to change the situation for participants of any timeframe. The price continues to march on but never gets out of line with values to the extent that owners are motivated to sell in order to take advantage of price away from value. Thus, price slowly and steadily leads values and value. This is able to occur in the housing market because people have a need for their house other than as an investment, and consumption of shelter is not easily decreased.

But in markets where the only need for the item is an economic need, and demand is relatively elastic, markets do not trend as predictably for as long a time. The price of oil over the course of the 1970s and 1980s, for example, demonstrates price leading value over a long timeframe, but value not following, and instead pulling price back down — in other words, corrective market action. Specifically, price rises in the 1970s were too dramatic. The velocity of change was so great that it affected the behavior of participants. The higher prices motivated enough long timeframe oil producers to explore, pump, and refine, particularly when governments provided tax incentives to encourage exploration and greater production.

The velocity of change also motivated buyers to cut back on their oil consumption. The Western world started conserving energy as governmental policy also discouraged consumption.

Both supply and demand were influenced by the entrance of long timeframe participants motivated by factors tied directly to the dramatic velocity of price change, thus ending the overpriced situation. The oil market was unable to continue in a strong bull market because price moved far enough from value to change the situation, encouraging production of oil for many timeframe participants while discouraging its consumption.

Thus, a stable trend comes only with relatively slow, relatively small incremental changes in which price moves slowly enough to pull value along with it. While markets can accept or digest a small price change over time, a relatively large price change over time cannot be accepted or digested, since it encourages market entry by those who have the power to end its acceptance or digestion. (Note: at the top or exhaustion point of a trend, incremental changes do not come slowly or in small doses.)

Only those who *have to buy* (short timeframe participants) will buy. Thus, activity must slow as long timeframe traders, *who have a choice,* sell, rejecting price as too far above value. In order for a trending market to stop and get market activity back to normal (a trading range), price must move far enough in the trending direction to attract long timeframe participants to stop the activity causing the trend (i.e., long timeframe buyers buying from short timeframe sellers).

Volatility

Volatility is a much misunderstood market factor, but can be explained and understood using market logic. It exists to a greater or lesser extent in all markets. Each continually produces a series of boom and bust excesses, vacillations which can be controlled or halted only by longer timeframe participants entering or short timeframe participants lengthening their timeframe. When there is diminished long timeframe influence (or when the market is trading only in one timeframe), market activity is very volatile. Thus, the volatility of a marketplace — the measure of the degree of vacillation between high and low in a market — is a function of the mix of timeframe perspective of the participants: markets become very volatile when participants are increasingly trading in the short term, the nearest timeframe. In other words, the tendency for long timeframe participants to shorten their timeframe triggers increased volatility, because their ability to buffer the market is diminished.

Illustrating volatility can be accomplished within the framework of a futures marketplace. You have already read that price is used to promote activity and time contains this activity. This means that as the market initially seeks an area that facilitates trade, this area is bounded by other timeframe buyers and sellers, each group responding oppositely to the market-created opportunities presented. As the market moves higher, it creates a selling opportunity for the other timeframe seller. At the opposite end of the range, lower prices create a buying opportunity for other timeframe buyers. As the response of either the other timeframe buyer or seller, or both the other timeframe buyer and seller — the market's buffer from price moving too drastically away from value — changes, volatility will be greater or less in one or both directions.

Thus, the market is most volatile when the condition of the market dictates that there is only one timeframe. In this instance, as dominant participants initiate positions in the market, all participants seek to initiate in the same direction, either buying or selling, thereby causing wide, volatile price swings.

In early market development, in seeking to find the initial balance area, day timeframe traders move the market directionally for the purpose of arresting the momentum causing the directional impact. They do this to give the market time for orderly trade. They are trying to find other timeframe traders willing to respond to this excess, this market-created opportunity to further impede the directional impact temporarily. The response of the other timeframe trader will be sporadic throughout the remaining time period. Lacking any evidence of trade of this nature, the market continues to proceed, producing a much wider range in order to shut off this directional impact more severely.

This illustrates the second point: that the market uses timeframe control in order to buffer the excess, and failing this, the excess continues, increasing volatility. When all participants are trading in a single timeframe, usually all act the same way at the same time and tremendous volatility ensues.

The Dominant Concern

By definition, a free market allows any participant who wants to buy, to buy, and any participant who wants to sell, to sell, regardless of the motive or quantity. In order to be able to do this, in every market at any given moment there is a dominant concern for the dominant (almost always short) timeframe, either producer or consumer participants, or both. The dominant concern is merely the news item that is the predominant focus or preoccupation of the short timeframe participants. It is usually a news event covered in the financial press and portrayed as the cause of recent market movement. The dominant concern is thus viewed as the culprit, the reason behind the recent market activity. But in reality, the process of the short timeframe participant needing to focus on and neutralize the current dominant concern by definition sets the price area of the market.

In other words, the dominant concern needs to be neutralized in the shortest timeframe as price seeks a balancing level for those participants who have to commit in the short term. Price neutralizes the market's dominant concern at that particular moment, facilitating trade by readjusting. In other words, the dominant concern must always be neutralized in the market's closest timeframe in order to facilitate trade. Thus, the market is always making the situation fair to both buyers and sellers operating in the shortest timeframe. For example, if a sudden plethora of buyers enters the market because of a drought, Federal intervention, etc., their reasons for doing so — or, if these are unknown to the market, then the simple fact of their doing so — will be the dominant concern that the short timeframe trader focuses on as he bids the market up.

The marketplace will continue to neutralize the most recent dominant concern until price gets far enough away from value so that a new concern, usually that of a longer timeframe, becomes dominant. These concerns can be continuous in nature or opposite in nature. This is a balancing process and is a part of the auction market process. In active auction markets, this balancing process is often rapid and volatile.

It is important to acknowledge that news and other concerns motivate the short timeframe participants, those who are the vast majority of a given day's, week's, or month's transactions. In other words, in neutralizing the dominant concern, the market as a whole overweights it. Thus, it is often from short timeframe participants focusing on the dominant concern that the market creates what is seen later as a temporary price excess. In other words, while the dominant concern is always discounted or neutralized, it is not always the concern of the long timeframe participants — those who buffer the market from getting too far away from value.

Formulating a Market Understanding

Understanding market logic will help every participant boost his likelihood of being successful in the market because he will be able to read market activity and receive market-generated information, information that few participants acknowledge or understand. This information specifically relates to how the market is accepting or rejecting higher or lower values over time. Here is the breakthrough upon which all market understanding is based: regardless of the market — organized or not — market activity is readable and can be studied and understood.

How does understanding the composition of market activity, the concept of timeframes, volatility, the dominant concern, etc., aid an individual in gaining a market understanding by reading market-generated information? The answer is, it does not — not without a framework from which to observe how each element comes together to impact market activity.

Such a framework would allow any individual to break down market activity into groupings of participant activity, that is, activity by the various participants as distinguished by their timeframes. Once activity can be distinguished by the timeframe of the participant who is active/inactive, known areas of operation and characteristics of the various timeframe groups can be distinguished. In other words, a sound framework for reading and analyzing the market will allow any individual to be able to isolate each of the kinds or categories of participant by their timeframe, thereby being able to distinguish type of market activity and to attribute conditions of the market to the proper participants, thus reading the market and understanding it.

Such a framework employs normal distribution, the bell curve, a tool which arranges and organizes data, presenting it in a readable format. Arranging market activity in such a way is straightforward. The length of time being studied is broken up into equal time units, each distinguished by a letter of the alphabet starting with A. Thus, price is the vertical axis and time the horizontal axis.

A Logical Framework for Observing Market Behavior

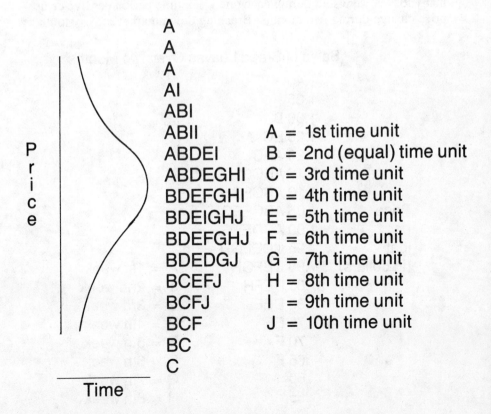

A = 1st time unit
B = 2nd (equal) time unit
C = 3rd time unit
D = 4th time unit
E = 5th time unit
F = 6th time unit
G = 7th time unit
H = 8th time unit
I = 9th time unit
J = 10th time unit

An illustration of time-price opportunities and of how they collectively define market activity, providing market information when arranged in a bell curve format, can be seen in a grocery store which sells bread. During market hours over the course of every day, week and month, a range of opportunities in time exist during which anyone can act as a buyer of bread and during which the store is acting as seller. Meanwhile, over the course of the month, week, and possibly the day, a range of prices charged for the bread is shifting to accommodate the needs and goals of the grocer. These changes in price are either accepted or rejected by consumers depending on their needs. The result of these two interests produce an area where the majority of trade takes place.

For example, at the beginning of the day, when bread is the freshest, the grocery may seek to charge "top dollar," whereas later into the day, the grocer may be forced to reduce the price substantially if he wishes to unload the day-old bread. To study the time-price opportunities in the bread market over the very short term — say one day's activity — one could monitor how many loaves were sold during each half hour time period per one cent price change during the day. Over the very long term — say two month's activity — one could monitor how many loaves were sold during each one week time period per five cent price change during two months. Breaking down market activity to its

Sales of Bread Loaves Over Two Months

	1.40	
	1.35	
	1.30 B	
	1.25 BC	
	1.20 ABC	
	1.15 ABCGH	
	1.10 ABCFGH	
Price	1.05 ABCEFGH	
per	1.00 ACDEFGH	
loaf	.95 CDEFGH	
(in dollars)	.90 DEFGH	A = 1st week
	.85 DEFH	B = 2nd week
	.80 DEF	C = 3rd week
	.75 EF	D = 4th week
	.70 F	E = 5th week
	.65 F	F = 6th week
	.60	G = 7th week
	.55	H = 8th week

basics — a range of time and price opportunities that are accepted or rejected by market participants — allows one to examine market activity. In this example, examining time-price relationships in the bread market yields information (temporary in nature) as to how the consumer has accepted the changes in bread price over time as demonstrated in volume of transaction within the higher versus lower price range.

A Trader-Investor in an Everyday Market

Generally speaking, people succeed in satisfying their everyday needs in non-organized non-exchange marketplaces such as food and clothing stores. This is because they make an effort to understand the particular market through the information it transmits. In doing so, they enable themselves to generate buy-sell decisions in a confident, independent manner. Yet few people are able to satisfy their needs when involved in an organized exchange marketplace, simply because people do not approach the more complex marketplace in the same way they approach the everyday marketplace; they do not feel confident doing their own thinking.

Every functioning marketplace provides information to participants as the market's activity relates to their particular needs. This information is very useful and applicable to any participant making buy-sell decisions, much more so than what could be termed fundamental information, information outside market activity. In other words, relating outside information to the market with the hope of generating buy-sell decisions is much more difficult than using the information the market provides to generate those decisions.

However, the information that every market provides is usually ignored or misunderstood when offered in the context of an organized exchange marketplace. Nevertheless, it is pivotal to supporting decisions which all participants must regularly make in order to fulfill individual goals. This information provides a known from which one must operate, using that known as what it is — temporary information — while monitoring forward market behavior for change. While this is very easy to do in simple marketplace situations, it becomes increasingly difficult as the size and complexity of the marketplace grows and as one becomes a smaller portion of market activity. Thus, the challenge becomes reducing collective market activity to bring forth its organizational essence.

The producer especially can gain value from understanding market information. In successfully marketing any product, there are many safe pricing strategies to employ in order to stimulate trade while maximizing profits. Repricing to maximize profits should be done only when the market activity of the product is already known, understood

Situation Indicating Acceptance: A Price Increase is Called For
          Number of units sold

Price	1st 3 days	2nd 3 days	3rd 3 days	4th 3 days
X	5	6	6	7

Situtation Indicating Acceptance at 2% Higher Price
          Number of cars sold in statistical sample

Price	1st 3 days	2nd 3 days	3rd 3 days	4th 3 days
X + 2%X	5	5	6	9

Situation Indicating Rejection at 6% Higher Price
          Number of cars sold in statistical sample

Price	1st 3 days	2nd 3 days	3rd 3 days	4th 3 days
X + 6%X	5	5	4	2

$$5 = 10,000$$

Assume that this car dealer's sales reflect a statistical sample size of all dealers. Assume that if this dealer sells five cars per three-day time unit, total sales across the country will match production. In other words, at five sales every three days, 10,000 cars will be produced and 10,000 will be sold.

and monitored. To understand market activity, one first needs to monitor time-price opportunities, the amount of transactional volume that occurs at each of the various price levels, formulated into a bell curve.

An Auto Example

Consider the pricing strategy of a marketing executive of an automobile manufacturer, a market participant whose goals are set out for him by a board of directors, company economists, etc. In implementing a program to carry out the board's desires, he listens to and monitors his market's activity, gains a market understanding as it relates to his program, and monitors this forward, making any adjustments necessary to fulfill his goal. This understanding of his market will help him more accurately repricing the product in order to sell the most cars at the highest possible price, thereby maximizing the company's profits. He is, in essence, a trader attempting to manage his trade in the short term from actual market information, and he is relying on the hope that the long-term program of the board of directors (based on information outside the market) is correct. When he communicates back to the board, he relates the market-generated information, not economic projections or his predictions.

If this executive is in charge of the marketing department, he knows that so long as monthly production — say 10,000 cars — is being sold, the company should raise prices in order to fulfill the goal of maximizing profits. He devotes energy to analyzing their cars' time-price opportunities — the number of cars being sold at x price the first three days of the month, versus the second three days, and so on. Are more cars being sold every successive time unit? Are fewer? If more cars are being sold every successive time unit to the point that total production of 10,000 cars is being sold, the market is showing acceptance of the specific model car at x price. Therefore, the executive knows an increase in price is called for. By monitoring the information the market provides, the executive is well aware of the market acceptance or rejection of the cars at the particular price over time.

The next month, after a 2% price hike, if the company's distributors still sell 10,000 — perhaps they might even sell 12,000 — the marketing executive realizes that demand is strong, and price is leading value. He knows that the company can continue to raise prices until the market's information shows saturation below the level of monthly production in order to maximize profits. He decides to continue raising prices every month, until the market's information tells him otherwise.

The marketing executive knows that price will continue to lead value so long as price is facilitating trade. He seeks to take advantage of the dominant concern, which his research may indicate involves the need for a moderately priced status car, or some other such variable. At some increased price, however, the dominant concern will be neutralized and a new dominant concern will surface. For instance, the realization may be made by the consumer that the moderately priced status car is not necessary. If this is the case, the price of the car will have gone far enough away from value that a new set of concerns becomes dominant. This might include, "For the price, I don't really need to make a change." Regardless, whenever the dominant concern changes, the transactional volume of sales as expressed in time-price opportunities changes quickly.

Sure enough, after three months and an overall 6% price increase, distributors can no longer sell 1000 cars per three days, which in the past projected out to 10,000 cars per month. Instead, the number of cars they are selling per three days drops to 900, which projects out to only 9000 per month. The executive realizes that the market does not appear receptive to higher prices by monitoring time-price opportunities. The executive concludes that at this point the market is not accepting higher prices as value and thus the product has been overpriced for the recent environment. The executive had to price the car too high to know the price had gone high enough. Once any marketer who is monitoring the market's information overprices, he knows it and changes, not waiting, but taking quick action. He realizes that the market information is telling him that price has reached the excess on the top side at the present. This information is an absolute temporary known to the company.

This process of monitoring time-price opportunities at various price levels is conducted for every car model by every company. Each company looks for the changes in transactional volume that occur at the various price levels for each model car, in order to decide how much production should be allocated for each model, given each company's goal of maximizing profits.

The assertions made earlier about the role of price and time in regulating market activity apply equally to the car market example as they do to all markets. Prices promote activity; lower prices promote increased buying activity among consumers and higher prices promote increased production activity among producers. Time regulates this activity. And price plus time equals transactional volume, market acceptance and value. For example, consumers associate the usual price charged for the specific model car with value. Those who want to buy it below value will have a limited opportunity when autos are on sale, characteristically, when the next model is introduced, thereby making the older model year less desirable.

Distinctions among Prices -- The Information Source

Each of the examples introduced demonstrates that all markets have an organizational structure which regularly produces a wide range of prices and hence a wide range of time-price opportunities. (It will be remembered that time-price opportunities are merely measuring units which differ from one another in that they denote transactions at different or similar prices, at different or the same levels of volume.) Prices, and hence time-price opportunities, can appear with little, medium or a lot of a relative amount of time. Those prices and hence those time-price opportunities that recur trade for a relatively large amount of time. They result in relatively large transactional volume and therefore display market acceptance or value for both sides of the market. They represent the marketplace establishing that time-price opportunity as a fair value. Thus, the greater the duration at a price or price area, the greater the value of that area.

In contrast, those prices and hence time-price opportunities which result in a relatively small amount of time result in relatively small amounts of transactional volume and display market rejection or unfair value for one side. Excesses of market price promotion which result in a range of prices are simply normal over- or undercompensations the market uses to find balance. Thus, all prices and all time-price opportunities are not equal, but can be distinguished from one another in terms other than price. In other words, the variance between

time-price opportunities, our defining measurement tool, is based on
recurrence over time. Time-price opportunities, and hence prices, can
be either accepted over time by the market as representing fair value
or rejected over time by the market as unfairly under- or overvalued.
It is the time-price opportunities that are taken or not taken or repeated
due to current conditions that provide the participant knowledge about
the marketplace. Thus, price, and hence time-price opportunities, will
be viewed in hindsight as either in excess or not in excess. In other
words, whether a price excess is rejected by the market as unfair value
or accepted by the market as fair value is an after-the-fact known that
becomes a reliable benchmark until changed.

Using these principles, the marketing executive for the auto manufacturer was able to read the market's preference of price based on
transactional data. He compared a range of time-price opportunities,
his measuring unit being the number of the particular model car sold
for x during each three-day period. When offered at the higher price,
if the number of cars sold during this constant measuring unit stayed
the same or grew, the executive knew that the price was being accepted
as fair value over time, since the market was demonstrating recurrence
at the price. After another price hike, when the number of cars sold
during the three-day period at a higher price began to fall, he was able
to compare the recurrence at the lower price with the non-recurrence
at the new, higher test price. He was thus alerted to a change in the
condition of the market at the higher price. In other words, he knew
after the fact that the change meant the higher price did not show equal
recurrence.

The increase of buying power versus selling power or the decrease
of buying power versus selling power will be displayed in the changing
acceptance of time-price opportunities.

All market participants are continually looking for an area to enter
the market at a fair or advantageous price, yet as demonstrated, only
the long timeframe participants have the ability to actually change the
condition of the market, since they only enter the market at an
advantageous price, thus causing change. Hence the market, in continually searching for an equilibrium area, an area of fair value which
attracts the greatest participation and thus facilitates the most trade,
does so through the market's process of creating excess while price is
advertising and promoting opportunity. In other words, price needs to
go too high in order for the marketplace to know that price has gone
high enough. Likewise, price needs to go too low in order for the
marketplace to know that price has gone low enough.

It was explained that market activity provides market participants
with vital known temporary information units which reveal the collective needs and goals of other participants as expressed in their use. As
we have seen, time-price opportunities indicate the market's trans-

actional volume over a series of fixed periods for a variety of prices. Thus, time-price opportunities (and hence prices) can appear with a large or small relative amount of time. Those time-price opportunities (and hence prices) which result in a large amount of time also result in large transactional volume and display market acceptance or value. On the other hand, those time-price opportunities, (and hence prices) which result in a small amount of time result in small amounts of volume and display market rejection or unfair value for one side. Thus, by examining time-price opportunities, the grocery store owner and the auto executive — and any participant of any market — can read the market's preference of the various time-price opportunities which occur at different times, at different or the same prices at different or the same levels of volume.

This preference is market-generated information which allows the participant to assess value. In other words, price plus time equals market acceptance, which equals transactional volume, which equals value. This is a definition of value which holds for all free markets. By separating prices out as seen over time versus prices not seen again, one can read the market's collective expression of accepted, rejected or changing value.

The logical conclusion is that any participant in any marketplace can now discriminate between prices, since all price changes are illustrated in market activity as time-price opportunities either accepted or rejected. In discriminating, one can discover any change in the condition of market activity over various prices over time. Viewing price movement over time as such, market activity is readable in that present market activity is monitored, and known information is related to changes in such market activity. This dictates the area where the market can facilitate trade at the moment.

Conclusion

Thus, while most participants believe that all prices are basically equal, an understanding of market activity allows an understanding of the behavior of the market, i.e., the realization that all prices clearly are not equal. The willingness of the participants to accept one time-price opportunity over another represents a collective perception of fairness or value in the marketplace.

II. Illustrative Examples

7

ILLUSTRATIVE EXAMPLES OF MARKET LOGIC

I n normal, everyday life, consumers are constantly confronted with what they may or may not consciously acknowledge as markets — but which nevertheless are markets. All markets — everyday and organized — operate similarly, in a manner explained by the principles introduced in the Chapter 2 outline. These principles explain all market behavior. Thinking consumers unconsciously operate based on an understanding of many of these principles. These principles — the market's logic, its operational procedures and its characteristics — after being presented in outline form in Chapter 2, have been individually discussed and illustrated in examples in Chapters 4, 5, and 6.

By now the reader should be aware that all prices are not equal, all opportunities to buy or sell are not the same. He should know that markets provide information which indicates the condition of the market, and extracting and reading this market-generated information is the key requisite to understanding a market. These are insights many a consumer already has regarding everyday market situations. In other words, before reading this book, many thinking consumers already had an unconscious understanding of the principles this book introduces in that they had the ability to understand simple, everyday markets, although they may or may not have been consciously aware of it. The value of understanding the principles of market logic on a conscious level lies in the realization that traders can now set up specific parameters which allow them to consciously monitor and analyze price versus value and the varied timeframe participants in the organized markets, as they subconsciously do in everyday markets.

The following illustrations will introduce situations which can help the reader further develop an understanding that all markets act similarly and all market situations are caused by the same forces. They will also help the reader develop his understanding of the other market principles, enhancing his ability to read the activity of the various participant timeframes, allowing him to understand on a conscious level any market situation.

Observing Market Participation in an Easily Read Marketplace

As has been discussed, all of us as market participants have our individual needs and goals which guide our timeframe perspectives and thus our activity in the market. We generally understand our needs and goals in everyday market situations, are able to distinguish between various opportunities which may fulfill those needs and goals, and are able to decide between opportunities by generating decisions confidently. Successful traders and investors are able to operate the same way within organized markets, applying knowledge of their individual situation, assessing the opportunities available, and making buy-sell decisions confidently.

It is assumed that the goal of every reader of this book is to be able to understand any market. To do this, one must understand the needs and goals which motivate the many market participants and determine their timeframe perspective. Knowing an individual's (or a group's) timeframe perspective is key to market understanding because market change -- price change through range extension -- is caused by the entrance of long timeframe participants upsetting what was an initial balance. The long timeframe participant enters a market which was previously balanced because he perceives price away from value: a market-created opportunity. It is only through knowing this that a market participant can position himself against the other participants in a risk-free manner. However, so long as one is able to observe participation in the marketplace -- and understand under what conditions such participation occurs -- it is not necessary to be aware of the "enunciated" views of the many market participants. One need only monitor their activity in the market, because the views and timeframes of all participants about that market are expressed in their activity.

A Hypothetical, Very Readable Market

The producer produces the product because the consumer desires it, either to use or to resell. While a centralized marketplace does not exist, both parties have an interest in facilitating trade. They have market-imposed timeframes (each can only conduct business when face to face with the other), they have participant timeframes based on their individual needs and perceptions, and both seek information about value. (The producer wishes to sell as expensively as possible and wishes to know how much the consumer will pay, while the consumer wishes to purchase as cheaply as possible and wishes to know how cheaply the producer will sell.)

Both producer and consumer are self-interested and observant, both have an equal opportunity to read and monitor the other's motivations -- but only as expressed through market participation -- and both wish to prepare themselves to read the demands of the other in an anticipatory manner.

If both adequately apply themselves to the task of observing the behavioral activity of the other as it is expressed in market activity, each will be able to anticipate the needs of the other and reach a mutually beneficial agreement. Since both seek to facilitate trade, extensive negotiating takes place. Each side tries to use excess price to promote trade. For example, the consumer may be saying, "I suppose I might be able to purchase 50 units at three," while the producer may be replying, "There's no way I could produce 50 units for less than eight." Time regulates this negotiating activity, and relatively little time is spent discussing price excesses, but, much time is spent haggling once the two get to discussing the price area each considers near fair value. This negotiation, as you can see, is an example of an active auction, producing a range of time-price opportunities.

The producer and consumer decide to enter into a agreement for the duration of one year. This agreement, while not a marketplace, is nevertheless trade and therefore can be viewed as a form of market. The agreement specifies that the consumer will purchase a fixed number of product units for a set price at regular time unit intervals. Thus, the consumer agrees to purchase a steady supply of the product while assuring himself a regular supply of the product at a fixed cost. Meanwhile the producer agrees to a fixed supply of the product in exchange for a fixed, steady profit. Both accept the price to be paid for the product as fair value.

This agreement illustrates the many factors which exist in a centralized marketplace. For instance, market activity (spelled out in the terms of the agreement) is triggered by market-imposed timeframes (such as the time it takes the producer to produce) and participant timeframes (such as the time units which would best fulfill the consumer's perceived need). A normal market's volatility depends upon the mix of long- and short-term market and individual timeframes. But, since the timeframes are fixed by the regularity of the time units, and the price is fixed for the duration of the year, both parties are operating in the same timeframes, and hence no volatility exists. Thus this "market" has demonstrated the ability to control and regulate itself through its allocation of price and time, yielding an agreement which produces balance in market activity.

Supply and demand considerations remain unchanged for the time being. All goes well, since the marketplace's market activity is in balance. In other words, the producer is able to meet the production need comfortably while the consumer meets the consumption requirements. On the contractually agreed upon date, the consumer comes to pick up and pay for his merchandise.

Each participant can examine and understand market activity by examining time-price opportunities. But since an agreement is in place for a year, time-price opportunities are not in flux, but are frozen. In this instance, there is no readable preference through variant time-price opportunities which occur at different times, at different or the same prices at different or the same levels of volume.

However, after several exchange dates have passed and business has been transacted as agreed, the consumer asks that the agreement be altered so that he can now pick up the same quantity of merchandise sooner, in effect asking the producer to increase the frequency of production. This would, of course, increase the producer's total production for the remainder of the year, a shortening in the buyer's timeframe which will increase market activity.

What has transpired? The consumer has shortened his (participant) timeframe, hoping to increase market activity. His reason: he has two timeframes, out to the end of the year and another over the short term. It is obvious that he has an economic advantage in requesting an increased delivery schedule. This act shows a shift in the supply-demand situation; the consumer is increasing his frequency of reorder, since he is gaining an advantage in doing so. Market activity is no longer in balance and hence, an opportunity for price change is evident. It becomes evident by studying the information provided by market activity as illustrated in time-price opportunities.

The producer is able to recognize that (since the consumer is shortening his timeframe) value is shifting, and he can assume that demand has increased, the best possible outcome for the consumer, and the worst for the producer — if price is held stagnant.

The length of time during which business was transacted at the agreed-upon price was reasonable enough — at least three transaction periods — thus also resulting in a large amount of transactional volume, thereby displaying that the market facilitated trade, indicating market acceptance or value.

Had the transactions occurred over a small amount of time, it would have resulted in only a small amount of volume and thus in hindsight might indicate market rejection or unfair value for one side. Thus, since all prices have the distinction of being either accepted as fair value or rejected as unfair value, and the producer's price has clearly been accepted, he should test the market by raising his price. Assuming he can speed up the production process to satisfy the consumer's request, the producer realizes that he is in a good position to raise his prices because the demand exists. The producer realizes that either the consumer's personal appetite for the product has increased or he has developed or is expanding his marketing of the product to others beside himself.

This would demonstrate the market displaying a price extension beyond the agreed-upon level. It is important to note that this price range extension (or simply range extension) was caused by a shift in the timeframe makeup of the market. The consumer shortened his timeframe, disrupting the previously balanced situation. This illustrates that while both had initially fixed timeframes, the consumer's timeframe change disrupts the balance. This unbalanced situation allows the producer to raise (extend) his price so that the the situation can be balanced.

Another example: if the consumer requested a drop in the frequency of the product, the producer would realize his need to cut production costs because the consumer was in a position to ask for a price reduction to stimulate more demand. Both of these scenarios are looked at in terms of incremental change over fixed timeframes. Any change indicates a change in the timeframe of the individuals, causing a change in the timeframe makeup of the market, causing range extension.

The consumer, in requesting an increase in the frequency of production, knew he was purchasing the product either at value or below value. If the consumer knew he was purchasing the product below value, was greedy and at the same time insightful, his strategy might be not to request an increase in the frequency of reorder, but rather to raise prices to his market without informing the producer, thereby withholding information from the market (where producer and consumer meet). Since the producer would not have to speed up or delay production, the consumer would have information the producer would not. (The consumer would be privy to information outside the marketplace and by not increasing his reorder frequency, would withhold market-generated information from the producer.)

The consumer could then wait until the original agreement expires. He knows something that the producer doesn't — that he could sell more than his agreed-upon allotment. He therefore should be able to negotiate a more advantageous contract with the producer — requesting a greater quantity of production delivered quicker, but only on the condition that the producer lower his price. The producer would have to look for signs outside the agreement (this artificial marketplace) if he were to protect himself. Such a sign might include new producers coming in, new producers not coming in, substitute products, etc. But in this artificial market environment, such a sign does not exist.

This example clearly illustrates that there is a vital information flow which comes from studying transactional data — the behavior of a marketplace. The consumer in this example absolutely knows the temporary information that he can sell more of the product, information the producer does not have. The producer must look for information outside the marketplace and apply it to the marketplace — a further step. He may or may not come to the conclusion which the consumer has come to. This clearly illustrates that there are two types of information pertinent to a marketplace.

The first type of information is derived from outside the market. The vast majority of investors and traders rely on interpretation of this type of economic data. The second is derived from the marketplace activity itself. Few investors and traders rely on it, but the majority of consumers do. The first type of information can be known by everyone. The second is known only by those who have access to transactional data.

This example also introduces the fact that whenever there is an unmatched timeframe change among a group in a marketplace, that change will cause a change in price.

8

SOME NON-HYPOTHETICAL, VERY READABLE MARKETS

T he following examples will take a very brief and simplistic approach to several everyday markets with the goal of conveying an understanding of three key principles of market logic, as they actually occur in these everyday situations and as they are realized by the consumer. The first is the equation, price + time = value, and its implications. The second is that all markets use price excesses or purpose prices to stimulate trade. The third is that the entrance of long timeframe participants extends the range, offering an increased range of opportunities to the marketplace and causing a more permanent change in value. (For simplicity's sake, the following will not ponder details outside this parameter.) It is these three principles which are the key to an understanding of price behavior, and hence to trader/investor decision making.

The following examples should illustrate how these three principles are universally grasped and understood by informed consumers making decisions in everyday market situations. In the following chapter, these same three principles will illustrate a market understanding in the organized marketplaces, thereby bridging the gap between consumer perceptions in everyday markets, and investor-trader perceptions in organized, exchange markets.

A Consumer Shopping for a Condominium

The situation of a consumer interested in purchasing a condominium in a large metropolitan city illustrates that price + time = value, and also some corollary implications. It is assumed that this consumer has the goal of making an informed decision (wishing to get the most for his money), and he has no immediate time constraints. In choosing which condominium to purchase, our consumer acts as most consumers do, unconsciously monitoring and assimilating market-generated information.

Likewise, the real estate developer – the other side of the consumer-producer equation – has the task of pricing and successfully marketing his condo units. To do this, he also must monitor his market and extract the market-generated information. In other words, both consumer and developer – whether they realize it or not – are essentially trading in a market. As market participants, their unconscious knowledge of markets will hold them in good stead, since the real estate market functions like any other. In other words, both have the ability to discriminate among price at, above, and below value, and both unconsciously associate a high time-price relationship (significant volume of transactions at a fixed price or price area) with value. Consider the following sets of circumstances.

1. The developer has set a price per square foot, and having measured and allowed for fixtures, he has priced the various size condo units in his building. But after an intensive six-month marketing campaign, he has sold only 10% of the units.

The housing consumer, as an interested buyer, has observed the relatively small amount of transactional activity over this period of time, and after viewing the complex with sales personnel, should realize that this price has been rejected by the real estate marketplace as too high. If he is interested in buying into this complex, he should assume he'll be able to successfully bid significantly lower than the developer's asking price.

In the event that he does not bid, or should his bid not be accepted, the consumer can assume that he'll be able to come back at a later date, and offer the same price. He can assume that *ceteris paribus* (static interest rates, static housing demand, etc.), he'll not lose out on this buying opportunity. In other words, he has not seen enough trans-actional volume at the developer's asking price, and since he unconsciously knows that price + time = value, he knows that this opportunity is an "overpriced" one, an opportunity to buy above value, and that the developer will probably be forced to lower his price if market conditions do not change, or else he will not sell many units. Thus, at this price in a static situation, the consumer knows that this specific opportunity will be available and that time is on his side. He does not have to initiate a purchase now at the developer's price. He knows he will have time to respond to this opportunity, and might consider responding to a lower price.

2. Consider the housing consumer's situation regarding another similar property within the immediate vicinity. This property has had the same six-month intensive marketing campaign, after which the developer has sold 80% of his units. Our housing consumer has observed a transaction volume level that indicates value in the eyes of the real estate marketplace. In other words, compared to the first example, this condominium property has been accepted by the marketplace as fair value. If he is interested in a unit in this complex, he can safely assume two things. First, he knows that he'll probably have to pay very close to the asking price -- if not the actual asking price -- in order to buy one of the few remaining units. Secondly, he knows that if negotiations fail, the opportunity to buy a condominium unit in this property will probably be short-lived. If he doesn't wish to purchase today or at today's offered price, he cannot expect that units will be available much later. The marketplace has valued this opportunity as a fair value, and time is not on the side of the person who waits in that instance. He must initiate a purchase if he wishes to own one of these units at the current price area.

3. As an aside to these two examples, consider another situation: one where the marketplace is assessing the property as below value, but price is not being readjusted upwards to balance the situation. How would the developer know he faced such a situation, and how would he handle it?

In areas where there is either a shortage of housing, or quickly changing market developments (such as lower interest rates, plans for new factories in the area, etc.), which increase demand and hence values, those developers who do not monitor market-generated information can not maximize the value of their product. Meanwhile, consumers who unconsciously monitor market-generated information often profit by initiating purchases, buying at what they know will soon be below value due to the changes in the supply-demand situation. They are in effect taking advantage of the developers' lack of information. While always pricing their product at what they consider to be fair value in the short timeframe, producers who do not consciously monitor market-generated information nevertheless cannot establish the market's perception of value. They often find that their perception of fair value differs vastly from that of the market. In the inflationary cycles from 1950 to 1980, this often meant that developers were selling housing faster then they had expected, but still below value in the longer timeframe.

Consider the way some developers handle the situation when the marketplace is assessing the property as below value, but the developer is unwilling or unable to readjust price upwards to balance the situation. Either units can be sold on a "first come, first served" basis, or a lottery can be held. In either case, since price + time = value, and price was offered for such a short period of time, the consumer can safely assume that the market is not at a fair price. Thus, one can expect initial resales to be at prices substantially higher than the artificially low lottery prices. Furthermore, if a lottery is the means of balancing supply and demand (rather than price and time), the consumer can assume that a high percentage of the lottery purchasers will be people who do not intend to move into the complex. Rather, they are long or short timeframe traders or investors, participants who take advantage of the lack of information on the part of the seller and are willing to allow time to work in their favor in order to make profits.

Consumer Awareness of Restaurants

Another familiar example of a market which illustrates the implications of price + time = value is a restaurant. A price offered over time which is not confirmed by acceptance of the opportunity does not equal value but displays market rejection. This type of activity in the market for preparing and serving food is illustrated by those restaurants which are consistently underpatronized. The lack of customers signals that the market doesn't accept the combination of location, service and food at the offered price as at or below competitive value. Thus, customers do not respond to the opportunity in quantity enough to keep the restaurant in business.

While underpatronizing signals market rejection (price above value), certain type of activity signals market acceptance (price and value equal), and another type signals what can be read as market ultra-acceptance, or price below value. Restaurants which take re-servations, eliminating the need for and existence of a line of patrons waiting to be seated, are probably offering what the marketplace measures as fair value. This can be assumed because of the reason a restaurant takes reservations: to have a chance at evening out the flow of customers through the dining period rather than discouraging customers. It is not common for restaurants to take reservations during those times when traffic will be high and demand will exceed supply.

A long line of patrons who are waiting for the opportunity to be served is a strong indication that the restaurant is offering a culinary opportunity which at the present is considered to be below value. Thus, the restaurant with long lines of patrons has the opportunity to either expand capacity or raise prices, or both.

The Market's Important but Temporary Operational Procedure

The assumptions which could be drawn by potential consumers of the condominium and restaurant examples were due to their monitoring a variable (price) against a constant (time) in a particular market and noting where transactional volume indicated market acceptance. This is the most obvious implication of the equation price + time = value. The second key understanding is the most important of every market's operational procedure: that price excesses or so-called purpose prices are used to stimulate or facilitate trade.

No market is static for very long. Prices are always changing, continually seeking to promote activity from other timeframe participants by offering opportunity. The market uses what can be termed operational procedures to facilitate more trade, using time as the controlling factor. Most consumers are aware of the operational procedures of the marketplace which cause temporary changes in price (excesses) to occur. They occur in order to facilitate trade due to the seasonal or cyclical shifts in the market's supply-demand situation. Using time as the controlling factors means that these excesses are offered for only a brief time and are by their very nature short-lived; if these opportunities were offered to the consumer over an extended time, they would become the new value area. Happy hour, below-market financing on new cars, the previously mentioned spring clearance and the high price charged in season at a seasonal resort, all are price excesses; their respective market's operational procedures exist because they facilitate trade. Numerous examples or more in-depth analysis are not needed. It is important to note that an excess price is a temporary change which does not effect a major change in value or the basic structure of the marketplace, but offers an attractive, low-risk opportunity.

9

THE MARKET'S MOST
IMPORTANT CHARACTERISTIC

W e move now to the most important part of a market's change, that development which causes a more permanent change in value. It is the entrance of a long timeframe participant who, in sensing a market-created opportunity, upsets the currently balanced situation.

The entrance of a long timeframe participant signals a fundamental structural change in a market and its effects are lasting, not temporary. Whenever a marketplace witnesses this phenomenon, there will be an extension of the range or pricing structure. Future value will be determined through the acceptance or nonacceptance of this new extension of price.

It is this type of situation which is both the most beneficial and most hazardous to the investor-trader. This is because the entrance of a long timeframe participant has a lasting impact. It is an event which is of obvious importance in everyday markets. Having this information has enhanced the consumer's ability. It will be the single event which will be highlighted in four markets: the auto and discount airline markets and two exchange-traded markets. The ability to extract this same information from organized exchange market data will have the same results as the ability to identify it in everyday markets. In all markets, identifying the entrance of a long timeframe participant yields a tremendous amount of market information. Being able to isolate and monitor this factor is key to reading range development and market continuation.

The U.S. Auto Market

The U.S. auto market of the 1950s and 1960s was dominated by Detroit's big four auto manufacturers and from a market standpoint, represented a static or balanced market situation. This market was balanced because it satisfied all the short timeframe participants' needs in a manner which satisfied all the participant needs. (The manufacturers prospered and the consumer was able to purchase at fair value.) However, this relatively noncompetitive situation of four companies, all building similar sized cars, while balanced in the short timeframe nevertheless represented a market-created opportunity for longer timeframe participants interested in manufacturing automobiles. In other words, Japanese manufacturers, notoriously long timeframe market participants, considered the U.S. automobile market as an attractive opportunity and decided to enter and compete in it.

They did so, offering a higher level of quality, substantially smaller size and a lower cost product. Prices for cars offered in this quasi-passive auction market did indeed move lower overall because of the new, cheaper Japanese models. In essence the availability of the lower priced Japanese cars expanded the range of purchasing opportunities on the lower end for U.S. consumers. Thus, the automobile market changed due to price range extension caused by the entrance of a long timeframe participant which upset the established balance.

Secondly, the U.S. consumers did indeed buy the Japanese product at these lower prices. Detroit's product became perceived as overpriced and of poor quality. Thus, since subsequent transactional volume was significant enough to establish a new value within this structure over time, the value area for all cars shifted down. The new value put the old big four at a competitive disadvantage.

U.S. consumers were able to discriminate between price at, above and below value and to act on a well-thought-out plan based on their perceptions of quality versus price. This change in value in the U.S. automobile market spelled a different opportunity for consumers. This possibly influenced longer timeframe participants on the consumer side of the producer-consumer equation -- those who bought a second car because of the low cost and fuel efficiency. Had the new products at lower prices been unattractive to U.S. consumers, the expanded range would have been rejected. Yet consumers responded to the expanded range, and the market shifted.

The transactional data are yielding information about the market's current appraisal of value, not only to the consumer who then was not as interested in Detroit's product, but to the executive in Detroit. The U.S. manufacturers, the former short timeframe producers, were forced to respond in a nonstatic way -- they built smaller, more fuel-efficient cars, offered 50,000-mile warranties, and increased the quality of their automobiles.

The Agricultural Marketplace

The evolution of the U.S. farm market from the decade of the 1970s through the mid-1980s, considered from a macro point of view, is another example of a market-created opportunity encouraging long timeframe participants to enter the market, thereby upsetting a balanced situation, and ultimately causing range extension downward.

The international agricultural market in the 1960s and up to the 1970s was dominated primarily by the American farmer. His vast international marketshare represented essentially a static or balanced market situation. This relatively noncompetitive situation unfolded throughout the 1970s. Increased demand meant high prices for agricultural commodities, high profit per acre and a relatively high level of prosperity. Farm equipment manufacturers responded by producing bigger and more costly machinery, and lending institutions in turn extended credit based on the increased value of farmland.

But this market-created opportunity caused the entrance of long timeframe participants. Longer timeframe participants not involved in the agricultural markets saw the balanced situation as an opportunity. The result during the late 1970s and into the 1980s was an increase in the amount of acreage brought into agricultural production, improved and rapid development and usage of seed hybrids, improved technology and research, all of which combined to produce more crops, thus buffering the initial price direction of agricultural products.

In addition, agricultural production in all third world countries was improved, particularly in Argentina and Brazil. Many governments at this time sought agricultural self-sufficiency and provided incentives to encourage such policy. Not only did this cut the potential U.S. export market, but it created several net exporters competing directly with the U.S. farmer, who now, while increasingly productive, faced a shrinking marketplace in which to sell.

Thus, the long timeframe participants saw the market-created opportunity and entered the market, inevitably causing range extension to the low end. In other words, price away from value over the long time frame attracted the entry into the marketplace of long timeframe participants, which then changed the condition of the marketplace.

A Grocery Marketplace

Consider how a corner grocery store's market for customers is affected by the entrance of a long timeframe participant, another grocery distributor.

The grocery store's market structure is that of a passive auction. The grocer provides a range of prices for differing quality of similar products, and for product substitutes from which the consumer can choose. Within this structure, the time-price opportunities accepted and rejected reveal to both consumer and producer-distributor extensive market-generated information as to how the market is performing. The consumer wants to purchase at a fair price and will do so on a continuing basis at a price where he has purchased in the past. Likewise, the owner will restock inventory based on the consumer's usage of products within this structure.

In a situation where the grocer is in a monopoly situation, most business is transacted at fair prices for the day timeframe. In other words, both consumer and producer feel price fulfills their need, but the grocer feels no need to offer excess prices in order to facilitate an increased amount of trade. His location and lack of competition encourage him to operate as a short timeframe participant. It is only when the situation changes that this pattern might be disrupted.

How this situation can change and how the consumer would handle a change is illustrated by the results of the opening of a nearby supermarket chain. In other words, this balanced market situation can change because of a change in the customer and grocer timeframe makeup, a change which would be caused by the entrance of longer timeframe participants who view the current balanced market structure as a market-created opportunity.

Consider how a new, competing store would change things: a new store would be built only if the longer timeframe grocers feel they can respond to a market-created opportunity. Since they are currently outside the marketplace and would sustain building costs to enter it, they view it not from the day timeframe, but from a longer timeframe.

If a supermarket branch sets up near the corner grocer, the new competition is going to influence the range of the first grocer's passive auction, causing a more complex situation than the formerly static one, and offering opportunity to the customer who is aware. All consumers who see the announcements and advertisements and notice the physical building going up (information outside the market) know that they will be able to take advantage of the competition. The corner store owner, too, realizes that he'll have to change his approach to the marketplace.

This is because the new store is going to offer purpose pricing to get customers into the store, causing many of them to lengthen their timeframe. In other words, because of the entrance of the longer timeframe participant, each store will be forced to offer purpose pricing in order to compete for the consumers.

Once the second store is opened for business, this new timeframe change will be expressed in prices charged, market-generated information. The consumer will read the change in market-generated information and respond to it. Because he is now offered price away from value by the two competitors, he has become a longer timeframe participant, responding only to market-created opportunities offered in the name of purpose pricing. As the majority of shoppers become longer timeframe participants, if no new customers are attracted, the grocer with the shorter timeframe of the two competitors -- usually the smaller, less capitalized corner store -- suffers an erosion of profits and may go out of business. If the pool of consumers grows, however, both stores can flourish.

The Airline Market

The airline industry is another everyday example of a marketplace -- a marketplace not for a product but for a service -- which has been profoundly affected by the influx of long timeframe participants.

The purpose of the airline market is to facilitate the greatest amount of trade by flying air travelers in filled airplanes. As with every marketplace, the cost of the airline industry's service -- transportation -- is very elastic. Labor, interest, energy and airplane costs are the key variables. Despite the airlines' marketing attempts, consumers traditionally do not maintain a great feeling of brand loyalty toward airlines. Indeed, air transportation is almost a "commodity." Other than the futures, stock and option markets, an airline market is probably the most complex and difficult to read market that ordinary consumers (and the airline's pricing executives) are involved in.

An airline single market would be defined as the aggregate of various fares available at different times from the various carriers for transportation from a location to a single destination. In other words, the fares charged by each of the various airlines to the same destination collectively compose a passive auction marketplace which continually offers a range of prices. Travelers choose among the range of prices and decide whether to buy or not. The excess price charged for a one-way ticket is the variable each airline's marketing department uses to promote activity. Every airline market -- like every other market -- is composed of participants with various timeframes who choose to act or not on market-imposed timeframes, thereby influencing the market's behavior. Market-imposed timeframes are the take-off times for each flight and participant timeframes are the needs of the individuals needing or wanting to travel.

A static or balanced situation existed in the U.S. airline markets when the landing route structure and the frequency with which each airline flew was determined by governmental agency. The airlines and union members prospered while the consumer was able to purchase at fair value. However, this relatively noncompetitive market situation changed drastically with governmental deregulation of the industry effectively lowering barriers to entry. When this was done, the industry represented a market-created opportunity for long timeframe participants, encouraging them to enter. In other words, long timeframe market participants considered the market — with its high pricing structure — as an attractive oppportunity and decided to enter and compete in it, offering a lower cost service.

It is important to remember that the need of any business competitor is to stay in business and his goal is to gain in profitability and/or marketshare. A new competitor's first move is toward establishing marketshare. This can be done in only one of two ways: either by attracting new users to the market via his airline or by attracting the users already in the market, who are using another airline. This is true in the airline business as in any other.

While every new competitor's long-term goal is to gain marketshare, to do so the company must over the short term seek merely to facilitate trade, in this case by promoting ridership on its airline in order to introduce its service to customers. To do that, the company must resort to purpose pricing, the market's temporary operational procedure for facilitating trade. In this case, the new airline offered excessively low fares — prices at which the airline would not be able to make profits.

With the onset of deregulation, many new "no-frills" airlines entered the field, and successfully competed against higher cost competitors by offering such excessively low fares.[4] Travelers accepted the "no-frills" approach and the new airlines flew filled while the others lost customers and flew partially empty. Each higher cost competitor soon read this market-generated information and understood the challenge — retain or expand marketshare by offering a lower cost service or go out of business because the market is rejecting the higher price as above the value offered by the "no-frills" competition. In other words, as competition increased and the dominant concern among the short timeframe airline management became deregulation, each company instituted a plan to handle the opportunity/ crisis by cutting costs, thereby forcing each to become more long timeframe in perspective. Thus, the entrance of the long timeframe discount airlines and the resulting extension of timeframe among the formerly short timeframe sellers caused the airline market to experience a tremendous range extension to the downside. Fares plummeted.

The short timeframe participant airline traveler is the business flyer who has to travel on short notice and must consequently pay a fair fare. In other words, the business traveler often does not have the luxury of traveling only when special low rates are offered. The long timeframe flyer is one who may or may not fly (i.e., on standby) but by making a reservation several weeks or months ahead is rewarded with a market-created opportunity when he responds to the new, lower price. The long timeframers would be the students, vacationers and others who can choose to fly at any time and tend to plan and shop ahead and/or book "standby."

Both of these buyer groups extend their timeframe as a long timeframe seller's entrance upsets the previously balanced market and fares plunge. This is because the ensuing fare war is offering many attractive situations, situations where price is below value for those who book their flights ahead. Thus, when a long timeframe influence upsets the balance of a static situation, consumers benefit by becoming long timeframe participants where possible, further upsetting the market.

Because of deregulation, long timeframe airlines (sellers) saw an opportunity and entered the market, and in doing so became short timeframe sellers. This introduction of long-term competition will always change the balance of either the passive or active auction structure. The changed market situation in turn influenced further timeframe participants on the other side of the producer-consumer equation to extend their timeframe.

The entrance of the long timeframe participant and its effect in stimulating interest in becoming a long timeframe buyer has impacted the market significantly. The elasticity which was inherent in the airline industry's operations has been reflected in its pricing structure: when the price charged for a particular route moves up, demand for transportation decreases and planes fly with a larger percentage of empty seats. When airlines charge less and price moves down, demand increases, and planes fly with full seats. New competitors increasingly entered the marketplace, employing a "no-frills" approach to service.

The airline market is another which demonstrates that any substantial change in value over time comes from a long timeframe trader responding to a market-created opportunity. This change will not be temporary in nature.

Conclusion

The inherent awareness and market understanding that each of us as consumers brings to all markets have been awakened. Hopefully, the reader can understand why by studying market-generated information. In any and all markets, he can:

1. understand that price + time = value in the present and that he can therefore discriminate between price at, above and below value and act based on a well-thought-out plan based on personal needs. This leads to the basic understanding of how values change, and how significant these changes are to price direction in both the immediate and longer term.

2. realize that like the world, no market is stable, and thus changes in value will inevitably occur. These changes can be temporary or more permanent in nature. Temporary procedures used in the everyday marketplace have price away from value in order to fulfill the market's purpose, which is to facilitate trade.

3. trace significant, more permanent changes in value to the entrance of the longer timeframe participant responding to a market-created opportunity or a disaster as it relates to his personal needs.

4. understand why the ensuing competition must change the direction of either the passive or active auction structure of the market, which influences participants on the other side of the timeframe. Every participant involved in a marketplace should seek to be aware of the structural changes brought about by the entrance of the other timeframe trader because they will be permanent, and mistakenly thinking that a market will come back will be costly.

Before moving on to the next chapter, the reader should be well versed in a working knowledge of the principles outlined in Chapter 2. When this is accomplished, consider one or several everyday markets with which you are familiar and thinking for yourself, apply the principles to its interworkings. It is important to actively expend energy accomplishing this; doing so involves cultivating the less developed type of knowledge (as introduced in the first chapter). In contrast, reading this book only cultivates the second, but provides a framework for the first.

In the next chapter, the awareness and understanding of markets will be applied to an organized futures market. While the details of procedures and conditions in the futures markets will be discussed to a greater extent, it will be the market-generated information formulated for visual presentation into a bell curve which will be the key to understanding. That is, market information formulated in this manner denotes acceptance (value) or rejection, temporary changes in the nature of price and value, and most important, the entrance of the participant who can cause more permanent change in the structure of the marketplace. By overlaying this basic understanding, one will have a beginning structure from which to gain a more detailed and comprehensive understanding. This will provide necessary information, information required by those who operate in everyday situations as consumers. With this knowledge, one can develop the self-confidence in decision making akin to that of consumers in everyday situations.

[4] In order to have an informed expectation as to how long the company will be able to price services below cost, one needs to ascertain the company's timeframe. In other words, how long will the new concern be able to sustain the purpose pricing mode before running out of money? How much capital does the company have available to garner a presence in this market, and how likely are they to discontinue competing in the more competitive routes if they do not meet with success in terms of a high ridership over a short timeframe while in a purpose pricing mode? This timeframe question is important because while price promotes activity through excess, time regulates this activity. Thus, the airline that is not as well financed operates from a shorter timeframe. And in any market situation, everything else being equal, the long timeframe participant has the stronger position, since time is the long timeframe participant's ally and the short timeframe participant's enemy.

10

A GLANCE AT
FUTURES MARKETS

W hat do discussions of the interests of new companies seeking market share and of consumers seeking bargains have to do with investing or trading in the organized financial markets? As said before, all markets are motivated by the same principles, namely those enumerated early in this book. Futures markets are no different from non-exchange or "unorganized" markets, contrary to the belief of the academic community. In other words, price and value in the organized or so-called efficient markets are two completely separate variables. What it costs at this moment is price, what it's worth to each individual is its value. Thus, a price for a futures contract, like a price for a stock, a piece of real estate, a used car, groceries, etc., can be under- and/or overvalued. No futures market is ever at value for an extended period. Price and value diverge in futures as in other markets because of the nature of markets. All this means that individuals can indeed distinguish between prices and value in the futures market, gaining information in the process. Focusing on market activity, rather than price, provides a structure that organizes each day's activity. The market can then be viewed objectively, as either a market in balance or one which is out of balance. Once an individual realizes this, virtually all questions about how to trade or invest successfully can be answered by relating the question to an unorganized, everyday market situation.

This chapter is a discussion of futures markets as an example of an organized market, not an all-inclusive explanation of how they function.

It will be divided into two parts. The first part will relate how the principles introduced in Chapter 2 apply to the futures markets -- as well as all other organized markets -- illustrating how futures markets are no different from any other market. The second part will use 10 days of market activity to demonstrate how any participant can study and learn to read the market, discovering how the entrance of the other timeframe participant affects the market, where value is being accepted and where price is being rejected, and whether the value behavior is continuing its movement.

A Glance at How the Futures Markets Function

Futures markets mirror other active action markets in almost every respect. As auction markets, each futures exchange has a location, the most prominent of which in the U.S. are in Chicago, New York, and Kansas City. Participants involved in futures trading are either present in person or represented by others. Those who are present can observe transactional information, while those represented by others previously could not.

As with every other marketplace, the purpose of every futures market is to facilitate trade. In other words, the market will always go to a price area that will allow the most trading activity to take place. When a price area is not facilitating trade, transactional volume eventually dries up, and that time-price opportunity area is eventually rejected. Thus, if price moves to an area which is reoccurring over time, and generates significant transactional volume, that price or price area is fulfilling the market's sole purpose: to facilitate trade.

This makes logical sense if it is thought through. In order for the market to facilitate trade, participants have to volunteer to use it. But few participants are going to volunteer to make a trade that they feel is unfair. If it is unfairly above value, it will be sold because fewer buyers consider the price fair and hence, most buyers will refrain from their buying activity. If it is unfairly below value, it will be bought as the sellers use the same rationale. Therefore, if participants are accepting the price and therefore trading at it, the area of price activity represents value for futures traders in that timeframe.

The principle that every futures market always seeks activity is illustrated almost daily at different times in every futures market. An example might have the market down two or three cents on the day and the trading pit will be empty. At this point -- when the market's transactional volume dries up and traders leave the pit -- savvy locals will get out of their short positions. One of the sayings savvy traders rely on is, "Never sell a dull one." This means that the market participant should not go in the same direction as the market has gone in order for it to get dull, or when the pit empties out.

When the pit fills back up, the market will almost always move in the opposite direction to which it has gone to create the inactivity. The pit fills back up because the higher prices attract people out of the coffee shops, etc., and into the pit and into the market. Thus, when no one wants to buy a market, it will rally because lower prices aren't creating any market activity. When the market comes back up, people react to the higher price, thereby generating further activity. This is an observation few people — even those exposed to the futures markets on a daily basis — have consciously articulated. It is an invaluable observation, explaining why price extremes are characteristically made on low volume. When this inactivity occurs, the individual who understands market logic realizes that chances are the market has done its job in finding that it had gone too far for that day, and he can use that excess as a benchmark from which to trade the long side.

Market activity in the futures markets is composed of the interaction of time and price, a time-price opportunity. Thus, the best way of studying market activity is studying the range of these price units over constant time periods. Each time-price opprtunity unit provides the possibility for one or more participants to voluntarily act as either buyer or seller. Thus, time-price opportunities are flexible measurements which portray market activity in a free market.

Market activity in the futures markets, as in every market, is generated by voluntary participant use and is triggered by market-imposed and participant timeframes. Several market-imposed timeframes in the bond market might be the next Fed intervention hour, today's close, or the next release of money supply figures, this week's close, and the next treasury auction. Indeed, all options and futures contracts, by definition, have a market-imposed timeframe known as expiration.

The futures market and its participants have varied timeframes which force participants to make buy-sell decisions. In previous examples, markets have been examined by analyzing the behavior of the participants. This can be done by studying and understanding the needs and goals of each of the participants, from which one could gauge that participant's time horizon. On the surface, this approach would not seem to be applicable to examining marketplaces with many varied participants. But participants can be collectively grouped by the length of their concerns and their timeframe or time horizon. Thus, the market is made up of self-interested individuals and therefore is motivated by the collective dominant, and latent timeframe concerns.

Different participants in the futures market have different timeframes during which to make their buy-sell decisions. Those participants with longer timeframe perspectives have time to manage their inventory and actions. Trading from a long timeframe gives the participant time to act. The longer one's timeframe, the longer one has to make all buy-sell decisions.

In an earlier chapter, the percentage mix of short timeframe versus long timeframe participants in an "at value" or "fair trade" price area was contrasted with the percentage mix of short versus long timeframe participants in a "below value" price area. The passage mentioned why the short timeframe participants dominated activity during the "at value" situation, but noted that long timeframe participants entered the market in quantity and competed when the product was offered at a price the market considered "below value." Furthermore, it was pointed out that the grocery store would sell more product for the duration of the "below value" offering, but would only offer the product at a special savings for a limited time. This is typical activity in a two-timeframe market.

In the process of facilitating trade in the short run, the futures markets create opportunities for participants operating from a longer timeframe. Long timeframe participation is evident at an extreme (buyers on bottom, sellers on top) when the market experiences a brief time-price relationship due to the extreme. This is caused by the increased competition among the short and long timeframe traders for the same opportunity. This illustrates *how* price promotes activity: it does so by attracting participants not already involved in the market — those participants with long timeframes. This is evident in all markets. This realization is significant because when price attracts long time-frame participants, the condition of the futures market is changed. This demonstrates that certain prices bring in those market participants who are not active under normal or "at value" market circumstances. When examining the normal bell curve distribution found in all markets (illustrated in the futures market examples), one finds that the bulk of trade in the value area is transacted by short timeframe participants. One also finds that, as in other markets, long timeframe participants give futures markets control over their primary function by being active on the extremes.

As well as balancing the timeframes of participants, futures markets are also continually in the process of balancing the two distinct and competing interests of the producers of the commodity or product on the one hand, and those of the consumers who demonstrate a need for the commodity or product on the other. As in every other marketplace, the futures markets continually fulfill needs for both sides of the producer-consumer equation. When a futures market as a service does not fulfill the needs and goals of both producer and consumer, it ceases to facilitate trade. Outside "customer paper" is not attracted to the pit, transactional volume dries up, and the pit is soon empty.

Thus, every active futures market balances the needs of both sides of the producer-consumer equation with four components: a product or commodity, a need for it, price promoting activity through excess, and time regulating that excess. Each day during market hours, futures markets control and regulate themselves through their allocation of price and time, yielding a natural organization which produces balance in an active phase called market activity. The market's natural organization means that it is regularly going to have extremes that over the short term are too high and too low. This will occur over every timeframe — hourly, daily, weekly, monthly, etc. Thus, all futures markets, like all other auction markets, must go too high to find out that they have gone high enough and too low to find out that they have gone low enough.

Market Activity Yields Information

In gathering information prior to taking buying or selling action in the futures market, the majority of participants focus on information which, strictly speaking, is found outside the marketplace. This outside information would include news reports, government data, remarks made by influential officials, etc.

Few focus on the fact that market activity, price over time organized by a bell curve, yields market-generated information. Indeed, for an individual with a keen market understanding — the ability to read market-generated information — studying information outside the market can become almost extraneous. Furthermore, it is very difficult to apply outside information to the market in order to discover where price is being accepted as value versus where price is being rejected, whether the value behavior is continuing, and the overall condition of the market. (Outside information becomes important when it motivates market-generated information indicating long timeframe participation in the opposite direction. An example might be the market breaking on the announcement of a bullish report.)

All one needs in order to locate value in a market is provided by studying the information provided by that market, regardless of the market. In more precise language, by studying variant time-price opportunities which occur over time, at different or the same prices at different or the same levels of volume, one can read the market's current preference. Thus, the futures markets continually provide a range of time-price opportunities during which any participant from any timeframe can act as either a buyer or seller. The area most accepted is the area most often used, which, therefore, facilitates trade.

An earlier chapter illustrated that market activity yields information when it discussed how the automobile manufacturing company's marketing executive can study transactional information to learn how he should price his product to maximize profits. Any manufacturer that sells the entire production will raise the price a certain percent. If, after the price rise, the company is still selling the entire production, prices should be raised again. The trend will be for higher prices, as long as the price rise is not steep and the market continues to absorb the manufacturer's entire production. The rate of price rise will probably increase until the manufacturer stops selling more. This approach — monitoring sales at various price levels in the form of time-price opportunities, and looking for change — demonstrates to the executive how the market is accepting the company's product at various price levels, thereby allowing the executive to either raise or lower prices and production with the goal of maximizing the company's profits.

This allusion is meant to illustrate that the only way any market participant can know he is maximizing his goal — selling as many of the product as possible for as much as possible — is by testing market receptivity at various prices. In other words, when current production is being sold at a given price, that price should be raised in small increments, slowly testing the marketplace. At some point, the product will be priced too high, and then price should be reduced quickly. It is only when this strategy is continually employed that a producer can truly maximize profits. Any other management approach to pricing cannot be said to maximize profits, since the producer does not know how the product is being received by the marketplace. He does not have transactional data, he does not have it organized, and so he does not know how the market values his product.

This yields the already discussed realization: in the process of facilitating trade, the market always creates excesses. It does so because it has to balance buyers with sellers using price and time. We now can understand why the excess is made on comparatively low volume.

When price moves away from an established value area to another price area, one of two things will occur: the new price will either be accepted as fair value or rejected as unfair value over time. When price is not moved away from what may be an excess quickly, the marketplace demonstrates acceptance. If it is rejected, the price is to be considered an excess.

For example, if suddenly, due to some variable such as weather, Fed interventions, or any other factor which will have a strong short-term influence on the perception of long-term supply and/or demand, either short timeframe or both short and and some long timeframe traders will want to do the same thing — either buy or sell — and a big rush will ensue. Price will move quickly to neutralize the concern. The question now becomes: will the new price area become accepted as value through time, or is it a quick blip -- an overreaction by short timeframe traders that becomes a market-created opportunity for long timeframe traders -- and thus displays market rejection. If it is the latter, the market has generated a very significant piece of short-term information about the attitude of the long timeframe participant who accepted the price as an opportunity, causing the market to bounce back.

Thus the participant with a market understanding distinguishes among prices, labeling those which are representative of value and those judged in excess based on the duration of their time occurrences. He also distinguishes among prices based on the degree and percentage change of this price as opposed to yesterday's value. Again, the single most important determinant to taking profitable opportunities versus nonprofitable opportunities is to know where this value area is.

It is important to understand and be able to read the information that market activity yields because it is when price and value diverge that a defined market opportunity for profit exists. The greater the divergence, the greater the opportunity for profit. Participants can take advantage of price away from value by selling the market when price is over value in their timeframe, or buying the market when price is undervalued in their timeframe. Thus, attaining an understanding and an ability to determine value and distinguish it from price is necessary before one can taking advantage of those opportunities created by the market, those which offer profits.

The market has a bigger range of value when it is facilitating trade, since more market acceptance means that more participation is attracted. Price is trying to move high enough to reduce activity but is being accepted. Value areas with these larger ranges usually indicate continuation, since prices have not yet gone high enough to shut off activity.

The type of market activity can be further classified according to how its current position compares to the previous day's value area. In other words, today's market activity becomes more significant when viewed as it relates to yesterday's value. Today's prices can only hold one of three positions: above, within or below yesterday's value area.

Consider the other timeframe trader's usual behavior. Other timeframe buying activity can be expected at prices below the previous day's value area. Buying price below value is a characteristic response of the other timeframe trader; this activity would be labeled responsive buying.

Other timeframe buying activity within or above the previous day's value area is not characteristic or even expected and is labeled initiative buying activity. Since it is not expected behavior by the other timeframe buyer, this type of activity provides significant information.

By the same token, other timeframe selling activity can be expected at prices above the previous day's value area, since selling price above value is a characteristic response of the other timeframe trader and would be labeled responsive selling.

Other timeframe selling activity within or below the previous day's value area is not characteristic or even expected and is labeled initiative selling activity. Again, since it is not expected behavior by the other timeframe seller, this type of activity provides significant information.

Within these parameters, the situation will not always be clearcut, but market activity in a two-timeframe market at interim and long-term tops and bottoms should demonstrate first responsive and then initiative activity opposite the recent direction. In other words, when a market has topped, first responsive selling and then initiating selling becomes apparent.

With these distinctions in mind, an individual with a market understanding can see that market activity always begins to change long before the trend turns or the extreme has been seen. Contrary to popular belief, futures markets are like all other markets in that they don't "change on a dime." This is because change is caused when the mix of short timeframe to long timeframe participants changes. It is important to understand how profound this statement is: individuals with different timeframes impact the market differently. In other words, in the absence of long timeframe participants, the market is dominated by short timeframe participants, those who seek fair value. But when long timeframe participants enter the market, they are competing with the short timeframe participants for the same time-price opportunities and hence upsetting the existing balance in the marketplace.

The major point is that a market's directional change is caused by a readable occurrence. Thus, a change in market activity signals to the participant with a market understanding that change, not continuation, is occurring. Yet most participants focus on price alone and thus do not see market activity showing that the condition of the market is changing due to the change in the mix of timeframe participation.

Characteristics of The Futures Markets

In all of business, it is necessary to understand what it is one is working with in order to understand it and how it works. It is therefore no surprise that few understand how to consistently profit from markets, since how they work seems mysterious.

There is no mystery. All futures markets are essentially ongoing auctions in an all-encompassing sense. One needs to know the degree of underlying activity in the auction structure to determine whether the auction is continuing its direction or ending. If a large action is proceeding, information is generated constantly by the ensuing initiating and responsive market activity of the other timeframe trader. Information is also being generated concerning the degree to which the market is facilitating trade.

In simple everyday markets, it was demonstrated that if one can isolate and understand an individual's timeframe, his interests could be understood. While an individual's timeframe horizon is a spectrum, one can simplify the situation by classifying individuals into two participant groupings: those who have entered or intend to enter the market during the "day timeframe;" and those who do not, and thus are considered outside the day timeframe, in the "other timeframe."

The floor local, especially the so-called "scalper," is an example of an organized market participant who has a basic and very readable pattern of operation based on his needs and goals. His basic need, like that of all businessmen, is to remain in business, and since he must make a daily livelihood, he is more or less forced to trade every day, and thus trade in the fair value area for that timeframe, that day. He operates from the shortest timeframe, and is thus a member of the class of day timeframe participants.

Day timeframe participants intend to trade within the range, seeking a fair trade within the structure. Their trade activity dominates the value area and serves to provide information solely on the market's ability to facilitate trade. It is important to note the day timeframe trader activity as it relates to facilitating trade, as his percentage of volume is such that it is a true reflection of the market fulfilling this role. In other words, the market's ability to facilitate trade comes from the volume created by the day timeframe trader.

A second, longer timeframe participant is the position trader, the participant who does not have to enter the market in the day timeframe, but may or may not enter. This group of other timeframe traders is comprised of numerous participants with various needs and goals. They collectively do not need to trade every day, but enter the market seeking to take advantage of attractive opportunities, namely price away from value.

Thus, participant timeframes — and hence all participants — in the futures markets can be grouped into two categories: day and other timeframes. There are both buyers and sellers in both categories. However, other timeframe sellers seldom trade with other timeframe buyers at the same time at the same price, since a defined market-created opportunity for a buyer would be opposite that for a seller and vice versa. (When they do trade, the volume generated is not significant enough to affect market activity, and hence is immaterial.) This yields a volatile combination whereby other timeframe buyers and sellers are serviced by day timeframe buyers and sellers.

Auctions continue in the same direction as long as activity which is creating the directional impact is still present and evident. This is the activity of the other timeframe trader. Since his activity or involvement in the market is voluntary, and further, since this is opposite for the other timeframe group (i.e., other timeframe buyers consider an opportunity differently than would other timeframe sellers) and the marketplace needs to facilitate trade, it means that all participants — other timeframe buyers and sellers, and day timeframe buyers and sellers — will be involved in the market over a large sample size of transactional data. Also, as market values change, the activity level of the isolated groups will show change.

It is the change in the percentage mix which changes the direction of a market. The day timeframe trader tries to make a trade at a fair price for that day's timeframe in order to facilitate trade. Meanwhile, the other timeframe trader looks to take advantage of a market-created opportunity in his timeframe. Transactions generated by day timeframe traders usually are the vast majority of all prices on any given day, but do not occur uniformly throughout the range of prices. The percentage of such a day's market activity is generally 40 to 90%, and the percentage of transactions attributed to other timeframe participants is generally 10 to 60%. This percentage can be more or less at any single price. In other words, the respective percentage activity of each type of trader varies within the produced range. This is constantly changing in response to differing degrees of imbalance caused by the other timeframe participant, and the resulting adjustment of the day timeframe participant, creating four different types of day structures.

The purpose of facilitating trade is to establish a fair price in the day timeframe. The market accomplishes this by producing a range of activity whereby directional price changes serve two purposes: first, to halt the impetus of buying or selling, or to decrease the amount of buying or selling; second, to provide enough time for an opposing response so that a fair area for trade is discovered.

```
            9526 K
            9525 KL
            9524 KL
            9523 KL
            9522 KL        This is a Market Profile of a U.S. Treasury
            9521 JKL       Bond futures contract. The day's low
            9520 GJKL      (9502) and the two immediately higher
            9519 GHJKL     price levels display market rejection,
            9518 GHJKL     caused by a high level of activity on
            9517 GHIJL     the part of the other timeframe buyers.
            9516 GHIJL     This high level of OTF buying activity
            9515 BGHIJL    at 9502, 9503 and 9504 resulted in
            9514 BGIJL     increased competition to buy, forcing
            9513 BFG       prices higher. Note that during the
            9512 BFG       subsequent (B) period, price moved
            9511 BCFG      high enough to shut off buying, which,
   Initial  9510 ABCDF     by the end of C period, displayed a
   Balance  9509 ABCDF     balanced area until later in the day.
     Area   9508 ABCDF
            9507 ACEF
            9506 ACE
            9505 AE
            9504 A
            9503 A
            9502 A
```

Within this framework, a sharp price movement during the day has the characteristic of first reducing the amount of directional activity causing the change. This seems to contradict the statement that the market exists to facilitate trade, but does not when the motives of the day timeframe trader and the floor local are taken into account. A sharp price movement thus eventually brings about a discovery of balance, allowing trade to continue. The market is buying time so that the other timeframe trader opposite this price move has time to react and place orders to take advantage of this opportunity during the session.

The day timeframe trader relies on using market-generated information as a short timeframe benchmark. This trader is the most sensitive barometer of change. He is the first to react to a change in the market. This group consists mostly of floor participants or "locals," and has the characteristic of extracting an edge (buying at the bid and selling at the offer) for providing liquidity. The edge is a small markup or markdown in the bid and ask price.

Other timeframe traders tend to apply outside information to the market as it relates to their own situation.

Futures markets control themselves through the use of time in relation to the timeframe participants. The day timeframe trader effects the immediate balance in order to facilitate trade. The market has a secondary balance when the initial balance is changed by the other timeframe trader acting on the initial balance as a market-created opportunity. He takes action, either because he views the market-created situation as attractive for his own situation, or because the market forces his activity as his anxiety increases. The effect in either case is a range extension beyond the initial hour's previous high/low.

Markets: Organized and Defined

As stated in an earlier chapter and mentioned again in this one, the "chaos" of pit activity -- price activity moving over time, caused by the activity of the different timeframe participants -- can be organized into statistically measurable half-hour units. When transactional data are formatted into a readable form of order using normal distribution or the bell curve, information becomes readable.

This has revealed what is called the Market Profile, a real time tool that captures and defines the marketplace. In other words, it captures and defines the day structure of the market, and allows an accurate reading of the effect the other timeframe trader has in shaping range development. Thus, the level of activity and type of influence that each timeframe group exerts on the market can be read and understood when arranged into the Market Profile.

Isolating On Key Activity

By organizing market activity with the Market Profile, one can read and understand the cause of directional continuation, change or climax. Whether a market will experience directional continuation, change or climax rests on if and to what degree the other timeframe trader enters the market, as demonstrated in earlier brief examples. Knowing how this occurs is the key to entering successful (risk-free, as will be explained later) positions, mainly for two reasons introduced earlier. For one, the other timeframe traders as a group do not change their opinion on the market quickly. Secondly, other timeframe buyers do not buy from other timeframe sellers, and vice versa, and only one long timeframe group (either long timeframe buyers or long timeframe sellers) can be active at a price at the same time.

Consider the fact that the other timeframe trader does not have to enter the market, or he can enter, and can do so either patiently or very anxiously. If the other timeframe trader is completely absent, the market's initial balance area — market activity in the first hour — will be undisturbed. If he is entering the market quietly or patiently, he can overcome a market by consistently and patiently using price orders to overwhelm the market's directional impact. When the other timeframe trader enters patiently, he is entering on the extremes of the day, taking advantage of market-created opportunities. When he has a little more anxiety, he enters the market with enough force to upset the initial balance area, thereby expanding or extending the range directionally. In doing so, he usually removes a temporary known unit of information, one extreme established during the first hour of trade. When his needs are getting away from him and thus he is quite anxious, he enters the market quietly and consistently all day, upsetting each new balance area as it is formed. Lastly, when his anxiety is highest, he completely overwhelms the initial balance area, causing a new value area to be developed far away from the first.

As in all markets, but particularly futures markets where 4% of the contracts traded are actually delivered, almost all participants have to exit their positions. Once a buyer has bought, he becomes a seller, and vice versa. Furthermore, all are free to change their timeframes. Thus, once they are in the market, both other timeframe and day timeframe traders need to reverse their position. Where the majority of day timeframe traders must fight the market-imposed timeframe (the close) the majority of other timeframe sellers must then become a long timeframe buyer somewhere within the range of patience-to-anxiety. Either can change his timeframe.

In summary, the types of range development are shaped by either of the two timeframe participants in our group. As the degree of balance is changed, the control of the market shifts between these two groups, leading to differing opportunities.

Preface To Market Profiles

This concludes the first section of chapter 10; the theoretical discussion of how futures markets operate similarly to all other markets.

You have glanced at how futures markets operate in the day timeframe. Next, to illustrate all that has been discussed thus far in this book, ten days of market activity in the Chicago Board of Trade treasury bond futures market and the Board's soybean market will be examined. These two markets will be presented and analyzed in profile form. While other organized markets are motivated by the same principles and are simply variations of these markets, these two markets have been chosen because data were readily available, provided by the Chicago Board of Trade.

The discussion of the profiles will be presented in three steps:

Step 1. Actual profiles of transactional data will be presented. Underneath each profile, all the major information regarding a) how value establishes itself and b) the activity of the other timeframe buyers and sellers will be introduced.

Step 2. A running commentary will interpret a) how value establishes itself and b) what the level of activity of the other timeframe buyers and sellers reveals about the market.

Step 3. Points at which the market offered free exposure will be located and discussed.

The discussion of these two markets is a very simplified one. In other words, the profiles are not going to be analyzed from the standpoint of the short-term market-generated information. Instead, the following will isolate, extract, categorize and analyze only the longer range activity of the other timeframe trader, focusing on how important his participation is in influencing the condition of the market throughout each day's range. In other words, the purpose of this examination and discussion of profiles is to illustrate the impact the other timeframe participant has on both intra-day range development and longer term trend. It should be noted that the following profiles contain a great deal more information that will not be explained in the discussions that follow the profiles.

In order to extract this information, several logical deductions pertaining to market activity have been made.

Logical Deductions

The authors' deductions taken from studying the market within the context of the bell curve and distinguishing between the activity of each type of participant are as follows:

Any activity within the first two time periods comprises the initial balance. This balance discovered by the day timeframe trader reacting to any influx or other timeframe activity. Range extension is an upsetting of this initial balance. Extension of the day's range during the second half hour time period is attributed to the local or day timeframe auction, and is representative of the day timeframe trader's attitude. This is important because, as stated earlier, the day timeframe trader is the participant most attuned to quick change in the condition of the market and his attitude is of great informational value.

Control shifts to the other timeframe trader at the end of the second half hour time period. Subsequent auctions in either direction are defined by an extension of range beyond the first two time periods. It is obvious that range extension is caused by the other timeframe trader taking advantage of a market-created opportunity, upsetting the initial balance.

As the market shifts between the control of the two timeframes, it is important to note that the activity level of the other timeframe trader is the important point to monitor. At his maximum influence, where, as a group, his trade is nearing 60% of the total daily volume, one can assume that his influence in subsequent sessions will waver because the maximum influence is far above his daily average. By the same token, if he is doing only a small percentage of business, we can assume that within the market's overall purpose of facilitating trade, he will at some point have to become active, and his activity can therefore be anticipated. There will be situations in which the other timeframe buyer or seller dominates the market for an extended period without the active participation of the other timeframe counterpart. Still, because of the need to facilitate trade, the market must go directionally far enough to "end the auction" at around the same point the opposite counterpoint begins his opposite auction.

The purpose of reading market activity is to gain a market understanding, both for the day's activity and for longer term activity. To do this, parameters must be developed so that in monitoring the market, one has the ability to isolate, extract, categorize, analyze and correctly deduce from the following information: who (short timeframe versus long timeframe) is doing what (responsive selling versus initiative selling; responsive buying versus initiative buying), when (during what timeframe), and where (at what price).

To oversimplify somewhat, the key to entering successful positions is to know when the other timeframe buyer or seller is beginning to get active traders, and to position yourself in the market in that direction. Once the who, what, when and where have been properly isolated, categorized and analyzed, one can deduce the why, since a participant's needs are expressed in his market participation. In order to read market activity in the futures market, we will isolate, extract and categorize other timeframe activity, focusing in on and montioring four portions of each profile:

1. The value area and how it changes, both directionally and in terms of its high-low range. Monitoring this indicates how the market is facilitating trade. The range of value area as defined by 70% of the day's volume and its location (higher or lower than the previous day) are illustrated in the lower left hand portion of each profile. This information is important when one is considering whether or not the market is facilitating trade.

2. The high and low extremes of the daily range. They are examined to discern the extent to which the other timeframe traders are active at relatively high and low prices. Daily extremes are known locations where other timeframe activity is expected. Our deduction is that any time more than a single print exists, other timeframe activity is indicated. However, if the daily extreme is made during the last time period in the day, the authors do not count them, as this price level has not been tested over time.

Monitoring the high and low extremes indicate whether the other timeframe trader influences the change in value in a voluntary way by responding to market-created opportunity. Monitoring the level of activity at the extremes helps determine the degree of influence that the other timeframe participants exercise in creating change in value or trend. For example, other timeframe selling at the top of a day's activity indicates that the other timeframe seller is at least mildly active.

3. The occurrence of range extension. Monitoring this indicates the other timeframe participant's activity in producing a change in the market's initial balance. Range extension indicates that the other timeframe participant is very active, not only taking advantage of a market-created opportunity at the extreme, but also at lower prices. In other words, when range extension occurs, the other timeframe trader is upsetting the initial balance of the market, a more aggressive activity level than acting on the extremes indicates.

4. Lastly, the most complicated calculation: the net buying or

selling of the other timeframe trader in the fair traded time-price opportunity area, as measured by the time-price opportunity (TPO) count. This indication allows one to monitor whether other timeframe participation in that day's value area is net selling or net buying. Our determination of net buying versus net selling comes from taking the difference in time-price opportunities above and below the highest time-price price nearest the middle of the day's price range. A number above/a number below results. A high number in the numerator (top) indicates net selling, and a high number in the denominator (bottom) indicates net buying by the other timeframe trader. There are numerous complex explanations for this, but to illustrate simply why it is so, consider the fact that the market must continually adjust to the cause upsetting the balance of the marketplace. It thereby moves directionally in order to keep a fair balance and facilitate trade. The low number is the net adjustment number which shuts off the activity. When you have two distributions in a profile that are separated by a single time-price opportunity, it is clearly a trend day, and during trend days, the other timeframe trader's activity is very high. It is therefore not necessary to count the fair traded area in a trend day, as it is obvious that other timeframe activity in the direction of price is evident.

Further, these last three indicators (2, 3, and 4) will be categorized as either:

a. Initiative activity
or b. Responsive activity

Both types are voluntary activities, and monitoring the activity of both long timeframe buyers and sellers as they vacillate between initiative and responsive activity is the main information required to monitor the long-term auction process. Understanding each group's primary stance denotes the activity level of the large sample size auction.

This distinction yields tremendous market information and can be made by attributing the activity of the changing value area to the group causing the change. (For example, when lower values are brought about by initiating sellers, a response from buyers who are responding to a market-created opportunity is present but passive, and vice versa.)

The following analysis is put forth not for the purpose of illustrating day-trading techniques, but rather to present a set of circumstances to support decision making when one is working with a large sample size of data. This information is going to be extracted and organized so that a set of circumstances for decision making can be understood. If this can indeed be accomplished, then one should be able to distinguish between high-risk, low-risk and no-risk opportunities and relate each to one's own individual situation, consistently generating sound decisions.

US Treasury Bonds
Step 1

Trade Price	% of Volume	Total	CTI1%	CTI2%	Half Hour Bracket Times At Which Prices Occurred
78 29/32	378	0.2	59.5	7.9	A
78 28/32	1294	0.6	52.6	13.1	A
78 27/32	1462	0.7	56.2	11.4	A
78 26/32	6444	3.2	44.7	10.0	A,B
78 25/32	6778	3.3	57.6	17.3	A,B,E
78 24/32	12248	6.0	60.2	12.4	A,B,D,E
78 23/32	14878	7.3	56.6	13.6	A,B,D,E,F
78 22/32	13538	6.6	56.6	16.1	A,B,C,D,E,F
78 21/32	10542	5.2	60.1	10.6	A,B,C,D,E,F,G
78 20/32	14820	7.3	55.6	12.7	A,B,C,D,F,G
78 19/32	14026	6.9	62.5	15.4	A,B,C,D,F,G
78 18/32	14014	6.9	57.9	13.4	A,B,C,D,F,G
78 17/32	9584	4.7	53.4	12.5	B,C,G,H,I
78 16/32	12222	6.0	51.6	16.1	B,C,G,H,I,J
78 15/32	9268	4.5	54.3	13.9	B,G,H,I,J
78 14/32	4594	2.3	41.1	35.9	H,I,J
78 13/32	1410	0.7	54.2	16.5	H,J
78 12/32	2572	1.3	53.8	12.5	J
78 11/32	8702	4.3	59.7	18.2	J
78 10/32	9672	4.7	63.5	9.8	J,K,L,M
78 9/32	13552	6.6	64.1	11.6	J,K,L,M
78 8/32	9772	4.8	63.1	8.0	J,K,L
78 7/32	6284	3.1	57.7	16.1	K,L
78 6/32	2988	1.5	66.7	12.5	K,L
78 5/32	3110	1.5	42.6	26.8	K
	144418	70.7	56.0	14.4	A,B,C,D,E,F,G,H,I,J

70% Range of Daily Volume	78 14/32 to 78 27/32			

		% of Total CTI1	CTI2
Total Volume for Sep 85 US Bonds	204152	57.3	14.1
Total Volume for US Bonds	219568	57.3	14.5
Total Spread Volume for Sep 85 US Bonds	2296	39.9	19.4

7-8 Value area: 7814-7827
     Initiating 1) Selling at top
     Initiating 2) Downside range extension
     Initiating 3) TPO count indicates selling (trend day)

Trade Price	% of Volume	Total	CTI1%	CTI2%	Half Hour Bracket Times At Which Prices Occurred
78 23/32	702	0.3	59.3	0.1	I
78 22/32	3302	1.2	59.4	10.4	H,I
78 21/32	5716	2.1	57.8	16.7	H,I
78 20/32	6100	2.2	60.9	15.6	H,I
78 19/32	4226	1.5	61.3	7.3	H,I
78 18/32	3532	1.3	60.4	14.9	H,I
78 17/32	5970	2.2	55.8	14.7	G,H,I
78 16/32	6544	2.4	53.3	8.0	G,H,I
78 15/32	7790	2.8	54.8	19.2	G,H,I
78 14/32	9996	3.6	54.7	10.2	F,G,H,I
78 13/32	12080	4.4	54.7	8.3	F,G,H,I,J
78 12/32	12334	4.5	54.5	16.5	E,F,G,I,J
78 11/32	13094	4.7	55.9	20.5	E,F,G,I,J,K,L
78 10/32	22578	8.2	58.8	12.4	E,F,I,J,K,L,M
78 9/32	23150	8.4	57.8	11.0	E,F,I,J,K,L.M
78 8/32	16528	6.0	59.5	12.4	D,E,F,J,K,L
78 7/32	11490	4.2	64.1	12.1	D,E,F,J,K,L
78 6/32	12046	4.4	58.7	12.1	D,E,J,K,L
78 5/32	3782	1.4	54.0	5.6	D,E
78 4/32	2570	0.9	56.3	17.3	D
78 3/32	5682	2.1	63.9	16.2	A,D
78 2/32	5150	1.9	60.6	15.1	A,B,C,D
78 1/32	11020	4.0	63.3	14.4	A,B,C,D
78	21734	7.9	56.4	8.9	A,B,C,D
77 31/32	16764	6.1	61.8	13.9	A,B,C
77 30/32	13452	4.9	60.6	13.1	A,B,C
77 29/32	8536	3.1	65.5	6.7	A,B
77 28/32	6274	2.3	60.6	7.8	A,B
77 27/32	2882	1.0	51.5	2.9	A
77 26/32	1270	0.5	55.8	0.8	A
	203538	73.7	57.8	12.6	A,B,C,D,E,F,G,H,I,J,K,L,M

70% Range of Daily Volume	78 to 78 17/32			

		% of Total	
		CTI1	CTI2
Total Volume for Sep 85 US Bonds	276294	58.6	12.3
Total Volume for US Bonds	285482	58.9	12.0
Total Spread Volume for Sep 85 US Bonds	2648	65.6	7.7

7-9 Value area: 7800-7817
     Responsive 1) Buying at bottom
     Responsive 2) Upside range extension
     Responsive 3) TPO count indicates buying (trend day)

Trade Price	% of Volume	Total	CTI1%	CTI2%	Half Hour Bracket Times At Which Prices Occurred
78 18/32	790	0.4	58.5	9.0	B
78 17/32	5524	2.9	54.9	11.3	B
78 16/32	7546	3.9	55.1	18.4	A,B
78 15/32	13186	6.9	57.1	15.2	A,B,D,E,F,H
78 14/32	19176	10.0	55.7	15.9	A,B,C,D,E,F,H
78 13/32	18614	9.7	59.9	13.0	A,B,C,D,E,F,H,I
78 12/32	12600	6.6	55.6	14.1	A,B,C,D,E,F,H,I,K
78 11/32	16308	8.5	60.9	9.5	A,B,C,D,E,F,H,I,J,K,L
78 10/32	21420	11.1	55.3	16.1	A,C,D,F,G,H,I,J,K,L
78 9/32	21766	11.3	62.9	10.2	C,D,F,G,H,I,J,K,L
78 8/32	15728	8.2	56.1	12.4	C,F,G,H,I,J,L
78 7/32	7528	3.9	58.0	13.3	F,G,J,L
78 6/32	3790	2.0	55.2	6.7	F,L
78 5/32	2474	1.3	56.5	7.0	L
78 4/32	4140	2.2	65.6	6.1	L
78 3/32	2748	1.4	60.3	5.2	L
78 2/32	1760	0.9	47.7	28.6	L
78 1/32	4140	2.2	47.9	22.6	L,M
78	7980	4.2	58.4	9.6	L,M
77 31/32	3560	1.9	56.6	7.0	L,M
77 30/32	1340	0.7	56.3	13.8	L,M
	138798	72.2	58.1	13.3	A,B,C,D,E,F,G,H,I,J,K,L

70% Range	78 8/32			
of Daily	to			
Volume	78 15/32		% of Total	
			CTI1	CTI2

Total volume for Sep 85 US Bonds	192118	57.7	13.0
Total Volume for US Bonds	199140	58.2	12.6
Total Spread Volume for Sep 85 US Bonds	756	56.3	4.8

7-10 Value area: 7808-7815
    Initiative 1) Selling at top
    Initiative 2) Downside range extension
    Initiative 3) TPO count indicates even balance

Trade Price	% of Volume	Total	CTI1%	CTI2%	Half Hour Bracket Times At Which Prices Occurred
77 27/32	54	0.0	72.2	0.0	A
77 26/32	586	0.2	49.8	4.4	A
77 25/32	1458	0.6	57.4	9.1	A
77 24/32	1248	0.5	43.8	9.3	A,C,D
77 23/32	9590	3.9	59.4	12.8	A,B,C,D
77 22/32	19778	8.1	57.9	12.8	A,B,C,D,E
77 21/32	22622	9.2	65.2	8.9	A,B,C,D,E
77 20/32	21054	8.6	63.1	11.4	A,B,C,D,E
77 19/32	13936	5.7	59.6	15.9	A,B,C,E
77 18/32	9070	3.7	61.0	10.4	A,B,E
77 17/32	7360	3.0	59.7	8.8	B,E
77 16/32	3264	1.3	48.5	16.6	B,E
77 15/32	9914	4.0	57.1	12.1	E,F,G
77 14/32	10768	4.4	56.6	8.4	E,F,G,H
77 13/32	10964	4.5	60.8	12.3	E,F,G,H,J,K
77 12/32	20766	8.5	59.1	14.3	F,G,H,I,J,K
77 11/32	16752	6.8	62.1	11.7	F,G,H,I,J,K
77 10/32	12552	5.1	61.0	7.8	F,G,H,I,J,K
77 9/32	9260	3.8	65.1	10.1	G,I,J,K,L
77 8/32	9740	4.0	55.7	12.6	G,I,K,L
77 7/32	7740	3.2	60.1	13.2	I,K,L,M
77 6/32	11468	4.7	60.2	15.6	K,L,M
77 5/32	10592	4.3	54.5	16.4	L,M
77 4/32	4746	1.9	47.0	9.0	L
77 3/32	264	0.1	81.4	3.8	L
	175838	71.6	60.3	11.9	A,B,C,D,E,F,G,H,I,J,K

70% Range of Daily Volume	77 11/32 to 77 23/32			

			% of Total	
			CTI1	CTI2
Total Volume for Sep 85 US Bonds	245546		59.7	11.9
Total Volume for US Bonds	262212		59.8	11.2
Total Spread Volume for Sep 85 US Bonds	2692		60.6	5.0

7-11 Value area: 7711-7723
         Initiative 1) Selling at top
         Initiative 2) Downside range extension
         Initiative 3) TPO count indicates selling

Trade Price	% of Volume	Total	CTI1%	CTI2%	Half Hour Bracket Times At Which Prices Occurred
77 18/32	2314	0.9	58.9	3.4	A
77 17/32	3270	1.3	58.9	12.3	A
77 16/32	3808	1.5	61.4	10.8	A
77 15/32	10678	4.2	60.6	15.5	A.B,L
77 14/32	15846	6.2	57.3	10.4	A,B,L,M
77 13/32	13352	5.2	62.7	9.0	A,B,L,M
77 12/32	14360	1.7	62.7	8.4	A,B,L
77 11/32	5460	2.1	59.6	13.6	A,B,L
77 10/32	10866	4.2	55.4	13.8	A,B,L
77 9/32	15892	6.2	60.2	13.9	A,B,L
77 8/32	15094	2.0	59.0	9.3	A,B,L
77 7/32	6978	2.7	62.9	14.8	A,B,L
77 6/32	4134	1.6	44.3	24.4	B,L
77 5/32	5244	2.0	59.9	19.0	C,L
77 4/32	3306	1.3	61.4	12.4	C,K,L
77 3/32	2720	1.1	61.6	12.0	C,H,J,K,L
77 2/32	7946	3.1	54.8	11.3	C,H,I,J,K
77 1/32	9704	3.8	55.4	12.1	C,H,I,J,K
77	7452	2.9	58.6	12.9	C,E,G,H,I,J
76 31/32	11642	4.5	56.1	12.7	C,E,F,G,H,I,J
76 30/32	16404	6.4	55.1	13.6	C,E,F,G,H,I,J
76 29/32	17644	6.9	55.6	11.5	C,D,E,F,G,H
76 28/32	26388	10.3	52.3	19.9	C,D,E,F
76 27/32	11974	4.7	61.5	13.1	C,D,E,F
76 26/32	9476	3.7	58.3	9.5	C,D,F
76 25/32	10708	4.2	56.7	18.2	C,D,F
76 24/32	12312	4.8	55.7	9.2	C,D
76 23/32	926	0.4	48.7	13.9	C,D
	185018	72.3	56.6	14.1	A,B,C,D,E,F,G,H,I,J,K,L

70% Range of Daily Volume	76 24/32 to 77 9/32			

		% of Total	
		CTI1	CTI2
Total Volume for Sep 85 US Bonds	255898	57.3	13.4
Total Volume for US Bonds	271210	57.5	12.6
Total Spread Volume for Sep 85 US Bonds	2462	52.4	0.0

7-12 Value area: 7624-7709
        Initiative 1) Selling at top
        Initiative 2) Downside range extension
        Initiative 3) TPO count indicates selling
                      (climax trend day taken out late)

Trade Price	% of Volume	Total	CTI1%	CTI2%	Half Hour Bracket Times At Which Prices Occurred
77 18/32	2048	1.3	50.6	15.9	L
77 17/32	5544	3.5	69.6	8.0	L
77 16/32	5000	3.2	62.5	6.0	F,L
77 15/32	4754	3.0	57.3	9.8	F,K,L
77 14/32	13502	8.6	54.6	12.9	E,F,K,L
77 13/32	16464	10.5	55.0	7.9	E,F,G,H,J,K,L
77 12/32	18192	11.6	54.7	11.5	C,D,E,F,G,H,I,J,K,L,M
77 11/32	19368	12.3	62.1	9.2	C,D,E,F,G,H,I,J,K,L,M
77 10/32	22230	14.1	53.5	13.5	B,C,D,E,G,H,I,J
77 9/32	8032	5.1	60.4	12.2	B,C,D,G,H,I,J
77 8/32	4016	2.6	60.6	7.7	A,B,C,G,H
77 7/32	6038	3.8	61.6	5.9	A,B
77 6/32	7510	4.8	60.5	8.3	A,B
77 5/32	4396	2.8	66.3	9.1	A,B
77 4/32	4476	2.8	64.4	9.4	A,B
77 3/32	7502	4.8	61.0	16.2	A
77 2/32	2700	1.7	56.9	19.1	A
77 1/32	1974	1.3	60.1	14.7	A
77	3442	2.2	47.2	25.5	A
	115352	73.4	57.1	10.6	A,B,C,D,E,F,G,H,I,J,K,L,M

```
70% Range          77  6/32
of Daily           to
Volume             77 14/32                          % of Total
                                                   CTI1      CTI2

Total Volume for Sep 85 US Bonds        157188      58.1      11.1
Total Volume for US Bonds               165006      58.2      10.9
Total Spread Volume for Sep 85 US Bonds   3357      48.9      24.9

7-15 Value area: 7706-7714
         Initiative 1) Buying at bottom
         Initiative 2) Upside range extension
         Initiative 3) TPO count indicates buying
```

Trade Price	% of Volume	Total	CTI1%	CTI2%	Half Hour Bracket Times At Which Prices Occurred
77 25/32	606	0.3	48.2	9.2	L,M
77 24/32	5452	2.5	54.2	7.3	D,K,L,M
77 23/32	12830	5.8	55.2	14.4	B,D,K,L,M
77 22/32	14058	6.4	56.3	14.1	B,D,E,J,K,L
77 21/32	20358	9.2	57.5	14.2	B,D,E,F,J,K,L
77 20/32	30964	14.0	58.3	12.9	B,C,D,E,F,I,J,K,L
77 19/32	22642	10.2	61.9	12.5	A,B,C,D,E,F,G,I,J,K,L
77 18/32	23398	10.6	57.2	15.3	A,B,C,E,F,G,I,J,K
77 17/32	15360	7.0	61.9	11.0	A,B,F,G,I,J
77 16/32	12996	5.9	57.2	7.1	A,B,F,G,I,J
77 15/32	16212	7.3	53.2	19.7	A,G,H,I
77 14/32	14056	6.4	59.0	15.1	A,G,H,I
77 13/32	11488	5.2	56.7	8.6	A,G,H,I
77 12/32	9108	4.1	59.6	9.9	A,G,H
77 11/32	6678	3.0	56.7	6.8	G,H
77 10/32	3362	1.5	48.7	13.1	G
77 9/32	1340	0.6	43.4	43.4	G
	155988	70.6	58.1	13.5	A,B,C,D,E,F,G,H,I,J,K,L

```
70% Range          77 15/32
of Daily           to
Volume             77 22/32                              % of Total
                                                     CTI1      CTI2

Total Volume for Sep 85 US Bonds       220908        57.6      13.1
Total Volume for US Bonds              228754        57.4      13.0
Total Spread Volume for Sep 85 US Bonds   2329       36.5      28.6

7-16 Value area: 7715-7722
      Initiative 1) Buying at bottom
      Initiative 2) Both upside and downside range extension; both failing
      Initiative 3) TPO count indicates buying
```

Trade Price	% of Volume	Total	CTI1%	CTI2%	Half Hour Bracket Times At Which Prices Occurred
78 12/32	914	0.3	60.1	0.5	A
78 11/32	5006	1.6	59.5	14.6	A
78 10/32	7604	2.4	55.3	7.5	A
78 9/32	8628	2.7	55.0	9.1	A
78 8/32	7326	2.3	49.2	19.6	A
78 7/32	5528	1.8	61.1	8.4	A
78 6/32	7256	2.3	63.0	10.8	A,C
78 5/32	10162	3.2	53.2	12.4	A,C,D
78 4/32	13386	4.3	54.7	15.0	A,B,C,D
78 3/32	17414	5.5	54.5	12.9	A,B,C,D
78 2/32	17628	5.6	58.3	7.7	A,B,C,D,L,M
78 1/32	15056	4.8	52.0	13.0	B,C,D,L,M
78	5206	1.7	47.2	12.9	B,D,L,M
77 31/32	3650	1.2	48.9	16.1	D,F,L
77 30/32	13198	4.2	57.9	12.7	D,E,F,L
77 29/32	13584	4.3	58.0	14.1	D,E,F,G,L
77 28/32	20864	6.6	54.7	12.8	D,E,F,G,L
77 27/32	10408	3.3	52.8	8.8	D,E,F,G,L
77 26/32	14366	4.6	57.3	8.9	D,E,F,G,K,L
77 25/32	20124	6.4	56.7	14.8	E,F,G,H,J,K,L
77 24/32	21248	6.7	53.9	14.9	E,F,G,H,J,K,L
77 23/32	19052	6.1	54.4	15.7	F,G,H,J,K
77 22/32	9426	3.0	54.0	8.7	F,G,H,I,J,K
77 21/32	7452	2.4	50.4	15.4	F,H,I,J
77 20/32	19020	6.0	54.4	16.0	H,I,J
77 19/32	9934	3.2	59.0	10.0	H,I,J
77 18/32	7198	2.3	58.0	9.0	H,I,J
77 17/32	3214	1.0	58.4	13.3	H
77 16/32	972	0.3	49.7	0.6	H
	227414	72.2	55.2	12.7	A,B,C,D,E,F,G,H,I,J,K,L,M

70% Range   77 18/32
of Daily   to
Volume   78 2/32

			% of Total	
			CTI1	CTI2
Total Volume for Sep 85 US Bonds		314824	55.3	12.6
Total Volume for US Bonds		331990	55.3	12.4
Total Spread Volume for Sep 85 US Bonds		8615	50.6	17.6

7-17 Value area: 7718-7802
        Responsive 1) Selling at top, buying at bottom
        Responsive 2) Downside range extension
        Initiative 3) TPO count indicates buying

Trade Price	% of Volume	Total	CTI1%	CTI2%	Half Hour Bracket Times At Which Prices Occurred
77 27/32	7168	2.1	67.5	3.9	A
77 26/32	5974	1.8	63.3	13.7	A
77 25/32	4468	1.3	60.0	12.8	A
77 24/32	2420	0.7	56.2	8.8	A,B
77 23/32	2350	0.7	55.2	3.6	A,B
77 22/32	2512	0.8	58.0	9.6	B
77 21/32	778	0.2	53.2	18.3	B
77 20/32	528	0.2	46.8	2.8	B
77 19/32	7946	2.4	58.7	9.6	B
77 18/32	5826	1.7	54.1	23.7	B
77 17/32	1336	0.4	61.0	21.7	B
77 16/32	1762	0.5	42.3	23.4	B
77 15/32	1350	0.4	59.0	11.0	B
77 14/32	2528	0.8	59.6	15.7	B
77 13/32	1400	0.4	51.6	11.2	B
77 12/32	1116	0.3	41.4	5.1	B
77 11/32	984	0.3	62.1	5.8	B
77 10/32	4080	1.2	55.7	6.6	B
77 9/32	9012	2.7	58.2	17.3	B,C
77 8/32	10334	3.1	54.0	16.0	B,C
77 7/32	6358	1.9	58.8	12.6	B,C
77 6/32	13430	4.0	56.5	17.1	B,C
77 5/32	11640	3.5	55.2	12.3	B,C,F,J
77 4/32	15460	4.6	56.2	12.9	B,C,D,E,F,G,I,J
77 3/32	21760	6.5	53.1	15.3	B,C,D,E,F,G,H,I,J,K
77 2/32	23092	6.9	55.6	13.2	B,C,D,E,F,G,H,I,K
77 1/32	20822	6.2	57.9	14.4	B,C,D,E,F,G,H,I,K
77	15116	4.5	55.4	13.9	B,C,D,E,F,G,H,K
76 31/32	10020	3.0	60.1	9.0	B,C,D,E,F,G,H,K
76 30/32	6992	2.1	57.7	15.6	C,D,F,G,H,K
76 29/32	10502	3.1	55.3	14.7	C,F,G,H,K,L
76 28/32	13272	4.0	58.6	10.0	C,F,H,K,L
76 27/32	12928	3.9	58.5	12.9	C,F,K,L
76 26/32	8974	2.7	51.0	12.9	C,F,K,L
76 25/32	5252	1.6	53.5	9.5	C,F,K,L,
76 24/32	2960	0.9	59.1	24.6	C,L
76 23/32	4484	1.3	56.4	7.0	L
76 22/32	3474	1.0	52.6	9.5	L
76 21/32	3346	1.0	56.6	13.3	L
76 20/32	2130	0.6	55.1	14.6	L
76 19/32	8322	2.5	58.2	17.4	L,M
76 18/32	6470	1.9	50.1	6.1	L,M
76 17/32	888	0.3	50.0	0.0	L,M
	235438	70.3	56.1	13.5	B,C,D,E,F,G,H,I,J,K,L

70% Range   76 20/32
of Daily   to
Volume   77 10/32

	% of Total	
	CTI1	CTI2
Total Volume for Sep 85 US Bonds 334752	56.5	13.7
Total Volume for US Bonds 375510	55.9	13.0
Total Spread for Sep 85 US Bonds 6460	44.7	33.3

7-18 Value area: 7620-7710
        Initiative 1) Selling at top
        Initiative 2) Downside range extension
        Responsive 3) TPO count indicates buying

Trade Price	% of Volume	Total	CTI1%	CTI2%	Half Hour Bracket Times At Which Prices Occurred
76 29/32	2332	1.0	43.4	36.0	A
76 28/32	3706	1.6	64.1	11.3	A
76 27/32	2334	1.0	65.3	14.0	A
76 26/32	2716	1.2	59.5	14.8	A
76 25/32	4112	1.8	67.6	7.5	A
76 24/32	5994	2.6	57.3	12.7	A,B
76 23/32	8042	3.4	59.6	9.7	A,B
76 22/32	7360	3.2	62.2	9.8	A,B
76 21/32	7690	3.3	67.4	8.9	A,B
76 20/32	12276	5.3	58.5	21.0	A,B,K
76 19/32	10150	4.3	58.0	14.2	A,B,K,L
76 18/32	8132	3.5	58.3	9.8	A,B,K,L
76 17/32	6708	2.9	57.3	14.9	A,B,H,I,K,L
76 16/32	9422	4.0	55.7	16.7	B,H,I,K,L
76 15/32	11180	4.8	48.5	9.9	B,H,I,J,K,L
76 14/32	12838	5.5	49.5	14.8	B,G,H,I,J,K,L,M
76 13/32	11922	5.1	52.0	6.9	B,F,G,H,I,J,K,L,M
76 12/32	13334	5.7	51.9	15.9	B,E,F,G,J,K,L
76 11/32	20886	8.9	54.8	15.8	B,C,D,E,F,G,J,K,L
76 10/32	28452	12.2	56.5	15.1	B,C,D,E,F,G,J,L
76 9/32	10878	4.7	54.0	15.5	B,C,D,E,F,G,J,L
76 8/32	9380	4.0	62.8	14.7	C,D,E
76 7/32	10688	4.6	60.1	17.5	C,D,E
76 6/32	10246	4.4	54.2	22.4	D
76 5/32	2550	1.1	53.4	12.0	D
76 4/43	122	0.1	42.6	0.8	D
	164066	70.3	54.9	14.7	A,B,C,D,E,F,G,H,I,J,K,L,M

70% Range of Daily Volume	76 6/32 to 76 18/32		
		% of Total	
		CTI1	CTI2
Total Volume for Sep 85 US Bonds	223450	56.4	14.5
Total Volume for US Bonds	257734	56.7	13.5

7-19 Value area: 7606-7618
       Initiating 1) Selling at top
       Initiating 2) Downside range extension
       Initiating 3) TPO count indicates selling

Step 2 -- Running Commentary

The activity of the first day came from other timeframe sellers, who were present and active throughout the range. They initiated activity (disrupted the initial balance) and in extending the range, drove the market down.

The second day brought lower values following a sharply lower opening. The buying activity this day was the opposite of the first day's activity and was made in response to the market-created opportunity as perceived by the other timeframe buyers. This leaves the market in a bracketed area — a trading range — where other timeframe sellers are active at high prices and other timeframe buyers are actively buying at low prices. The key distinction between the activity of the two groups is that the buying was responsive (buyers responding to lower prices) while the selling was initiative (sellers were not selling in response to high and attractive prices, but were initiating selling activity at lower prices). In other words, sellers did not initiate new activity at the lower level, nor on the range extension opportunity offered to them. This is a good illustration of how a directional price movement shuts off a very strong known activity.

We've seen initiating action by the other timeframe sellers and responsive action by the other timeframe buyers. In trying to determine whether the market is in a down auction, an up auction, or a stalemate — a trading range — we can assume that any further initiating activity by the other timeframe seller will definitely indicate that the market is in a down auction. This is a safe deduction because such activity will mean that the market will have to go lower — as it did in the instance above — to slow down and eventually shut off selling activity.

The third day indicates selling activity at the top of the range and again in a late downside range extension. This is the initiating activity which clarifies the market's situation. In looking at the early profile, it is clear that the value area developing was small, and trade was not being facilitated, nor was the market building higher values, as this area was within the previous day's value area. The previous day's buying did not produce higher values than the first day. On this third day, sellers were responding to the fair balance by selling and caused range extension. The TPO count is even, but only after L period, meaning that prior to L period, other timeframe selling in the value area is indicated as well.

The fourth day, the market was lower with a developing value area and activity that indicates selling at the top of the range, again resulting in downside range extension and again in the value area, as indicated by the TPO count. This again is initiating activity at this new, lower level. Important also is the fact that the range of the value area was larger than the previous day, where trade early on was not being facilitated. This signals continued downside activity, since lower prices are facilitating increased trade.

On the fifth day, lower values developed in a similar way. The market showed initiating selling in all three areas. Successive activity from the other timeframe sellers cannot be sustained at this level, as their percentage of trade in this two-day sample is far greater than normal. In the first day of this two-day sample, sellers were probably responding to what then presented a market-created opportunity, and the second day the activity was probably due to a market-forcing type of activity which usually brings a temporary climax in anxiety. In other words, those desiring to sell have probably covered their immediate needs while they await an opportunity to trade at a more leisurely pace. We can assume that their activity level should diminish in the short term and increase only on a market-created opportunity such as a sharply higher opening. This is not to say that the down auction has ended, because activity which occurred is not indicative of a change in the total auction. In fact, there really is more activity at this lower level than there was at the higher level. Clearly, auctions end only when activity is ended, which is not indicated yet.

The sixth day brings slightly higher values in a narrow range. Initiating activity comes from the other timeframe buyer, who bought the low end of the range, and bought with sufficient fervor to create an upside range extension, and had buying in the value area. This is initiating activity because unchanged to higher values developed.

The seventh day brings slightly higher values. The low end of the range was again bought in initiating activity by other timeframe buyers. Range extension on both ends failed. The first failure brought an attempt to extend the range to the downside. When that failed to create activity, it probed the opposite side to find activity in that direction. When this also failed, the market took its clue from the fact that there was buying on the bottom and positive TPO count, and again probed for activity toward the top. For the second day of higher values, the market again has a narrow value area, indicating that buying activity does not facilitate the degree of trade participation that selling activity has done, thus leaving intact the assumption that the down auction prevails. The dominant force continues to be the other time-frame sellers; having satisfied their immediate needs during the past few days, they are awaiting the market-created opportunity for continued response. Looking at this day as a whole, it provides substantial information in that the market is in a neutral situation. Sellers do not want to initiate activity at these or lower prices (although they may be forced to) nor are the buyers willing to extend their activity any further than they have the last two days. The neutral day is determined by the fact that no net influence exists.

On the eighth day the market opens sharply higher, and the other timeframe seller responds by selling in the high area of the range, in the range extension, and in the value areas indicated by TPO selling. The higher and wide-ranging value area indicates that many day timeframe buyers were active and that their volume is greater than that of other timeframe traders. Thus, they had an influence on the day's activity, but important to note, this has little impact on the direction of the auction process. This is a good example of other timeframe traders moving the market directionally in auctions (trends) where price and value are opposite to the directional market activity that occurred.

On the ninth day, the market was lower with a wider value area. Initiating selling occurred at the top of the range and again in a downside range extension. The TPO showed a responsive buyer activity.

The market on the last day of the sample shows initiating selling at the top of the range, a downside range extension and TPO selling, all initiating other timeframe selling activity. Clearly, then, this is the lowest possible value area at the end of our sample, yet the other timeframe seller is as active as he was throughout the auction profile. Clearly, the down auction is not over as we leave this sample, because the activity of the other timeframe seller has not ended. This means that the first step toward ending the downtrend will occur when prices go low enough to shut off his initiating activity and bring about activity on the part of the other timeframe buyer, the participant who has been passive throughout this study. The initiating buying activity has never produced the wide value areas indicating trade facilitation. At a price level low enough, the OTC buyer's activity will begin to do so, and will produce more trade than the initiating selling activity produces.

Step 3 — "Free Exposure"

Consider the situation most attractive to the market participant -- that in which conditions are favorable for "free exposure," where money will either be made or not, but it will not be lost in any substantial way. In seeking risk-free exposure, the first thing to note is the type of auction structure in place. The bond market illustrated in the profiles is in a down auction, as established early on. This can be seen by the initiating activity on the first day and the lower values on the second. The unchanged values on the third and the initiated activity being taken by the other timeframe seller shows this continuing activity, and activity is what makes the auction process continue.

Positioning with this down auction activity — even as late as the close on this third day — is a risk-free exposure situation. In other words, at this point one needn't fear being late, because the other timeframe buyer is still not taking an initiating stance, but remains passive. (The auction process cannot change until roles are reversed.)

The opportunities for both buyer and seller are clearly not the same, since the other timeframe buyer does not trade with the other timeframe seller. The day timeframe trader does not affect the direction impact of the market, but only is monitored to isolate ongoing trade facilitation.

On the fourth day, the market has activity in all four areas, and is facilitating trade. It must go lower to shut off this activity and provides another safe selling opportunity. The following day the activity is duplicated. This is rather late for one to enter a move. This is not to say that selling at this point will not produce profits, but it means that being late necessitates waiting with the trade, because one is now working in the direction of the overall auction process, and that information supplied from the marketplace needs to reaffirm its strength. Sustained activity from the seller requires that his immediate needs are satisfied. A seller still is with the major trend, but the activity of the other timeframe buyer needs to be monitored closely.

All other timeframe buying to date has been responsive and the next day gives the condition favorable to buying exposure, even though the auction is presently in a down mode. While the value area illustrates that the market is not facilitating a great deal of trade, whenever this initiating activity occurs throughout the range, it is sufficient to enable free exposure due to the fact that it has to go higher to shut it off. All the buying activity was initiative, which provides enough activity for free exposure into the next day, wherein the market has to be monitored for continuation of buying initiation or else the position has to be exited. This is not to say that this situation is an attractive buying opportunity. The point is, however, that if one seeks to buy, this is an attractive place from the standpoint of minimizing "bad" exposure. Further, in the auction process, whenever initiative activity occurs in all three categories of range — especially with a confirming (wider) value area, one can assume risk-free exposure when going in the direction of the initiation.

The next day had higher values, but activity that was disconcerting for buyers. It was a neutral day, and neutral days revert back to the original initiative — the down auction.

The next day — with higher values and responsive selling activity dominating the range — offered the same opportunity of free selling exposure to the seller, regardless of when the position was entered. This was responsive activity in a down auction. Responsive action in all three categories means that one should be sure to be positioned with the major auction direction. In other words, responsive activity in all three categories in an opposite type of auction does not offer free exposure.

There is more activity at bottom than at top. The other timeframe seller is more active here. As the examples end, the marketplace is still in a clear down auction. Buyers can sit back and patiently await opportunities, selecting those which meet their needs. They are not rushed, nor are they interested in creating activity.

Regardless of an individual's trading or investing style, the market, broken down into segments of prices transacted in time and formulated into a bell curve, provides a set of circumstances available to read. Reading and interpreting the market in this manner allows one to gain an understanding of how best to implement one's ideas and needs in the marketplace.

The following are actual profiles of transactional data from Chicago Board of Trade Soybean futures from July 15 through July 26, 1985. Note that underneath each profile, all the major information regarding 1) how the market is establishing value, and 2) the activity of the other timeframe buyers and sellers, is presented.

Soybeans
Step 1

Trade Price	% of Volume	Total	CTI1%	CTI2%	Half Hour Bracket Times At Which Prices Occurred
580 1/2	730	0.5	71.2	8.2	E
580 1/4	210	0.1	61.9	2.4	E
580	4160	2.9	41.6	10.1	E,F
579 3/4	1020	0.7	53.9	1.0	D,E,F
579 1/2	8060	5.7	63.2	6.1	D,E,F
579 1/4	970	0.7	62.4	1.0	D,E,F
579	16880	11.9	57.9	16.6	D,E,F
578 3/4	2380	1.7	70.6	0.6	D,E,F
578 1/2	12720	9.0	64.4	8.9	D,E,F
578 1/4	2770	2.0	67.5	2.5	D,E,F,K
578	19800	14.0	57.4	11.5	D,E,F,G,H,J,K
577 3/4	5170	3.6	53.1	5.2	D,F,G,H,J,K
577 1/2	16050	11.3	55.0	9.5	D,F,G,H,I,J,K
577 1/4	7380	5.2	67.9	6.1	D,F,G,H,I,J,K
577	15000	10.6	53.0	4.7	D,G,H,I,J,K
576 3/4	3600	2.5	58.1	2.8	D,H,I,J,K
576 1/2	8870	6.3	61.0	9.1	D,H,I,J,K
576 1/4	2750	1.9	65.3	1.3	D,H,I,J,K
576	10680	7.5	56.7	5.0	D,H,I,J
575 3/4	40	0.0	50.0	0.0	D,I
575 1/2	2160	1.5	57.6	0.9	D
575 1/4	30	0.0	50.0	0.0	D
575	320	0.2	43.8	0.0	D
	101750	71.8	58.5	9.2	D,E,F,G,H,I,J,K

70% Range of Daily Volume	576 3/4 to 579			

		% of Total	
		CTI1	CTI2
Total Volume for Nov 85 Soybeans	141,750	58.4	8.3
Total Volume for Soybeans	220,220	58.5	9.9
Total Spread Volume for Nov 85 Soybeans	3,280	54.9	1.8

7-15 Value area: 576 3/4-579
                1) Buying at bottom, selling at top
                2) No range extension beyond first hour
     Responsive 3) TPO count indicates very slight selling

Trade Price	% of Volume	Total	CTI1%	CTI2%	Half Hour Bracket Times At Which Prices Occurred
577 1/2	10	0.0	50.0	0.0	D
577 1/4	180	0.1	72.2	5.6	D
577	3340	1.6	57.3	3.1	D
576 3/4	400	0.2	55.0	0.0	D
576 1/2	3950	1.9	55.4	3.8	D
576 1/4	2310	1.1	75.8	2.4	D
576	6240	3.0	74.0	7.8	D
575 3/4	1670	0.8	67.1	0.6	D
575 1/2	5650	2.7	75.6	4.1	D
575 1/4	2330	1.1	68.2	3.9	D
575	10030	4.9	70.0	4.2	D
574 3/4	1870	0.9	65.0	16.8	D
574 1/2	2400	1.2	65.4	0.0	D
574 1/4	400	0.2	48.8	2.5	D
574	4580	2.2	55.3	5.1	D,E
573 3/4	3430	1.7	62.2	1.5	D,E
573 1/2	6170	3.0	68.2	9.4	D,E
573 1/4	3380	1.6	65.1	2.4	D,E
573	4730	2.3	42.8	5.0	D,E
572 3/4	1830	0.9	70.2	3.6	E
572 1/2	1000	0.5	62.0	0.0	E
572 1/4	540	0.3	32.4	9.3	E
572	2370	1.1	41.6	7.2	E
571 3/4	980	0.5	56.6	2.6	E
571 1/2	2050	1.0	65.9	3.9	E
571 1/4	1040	0.5	64.4	2.9	E
571	3960	1.9	55.4	11.5	E
570 3/4	890	0.4	57.9	5.1	E
570 1/2	1700	0.8	49.7	3.5	E
570 1/4	920	0.4	37.5	3.3	E
570	2720	1.3	64.3	7.7	E
569 3/4	120	0.1	50.0	0.0	E
569 1/2	2720	1.3	59.7	2.8	E,K
569 1/4	1600	0.8	58.1	9.4	E,G,K
569	8530	4.1	63.4	10.6	E,F,G,H,K
568 3/4	3230	1.6	69.5	3.4	E,F,G,H,K
568 1/2	8740	4.2	61.2	10.1	E,F,G,H,I,K
568 1/4	4510	2.2	63.7	5.1	E,F,G,H,I,K
568	26670	12.9	58.2	4.5	E,F,G,H,I,J,K
567 3/4	7140	3.5	69.5	5.7	E,F,G,H,I,J,K
567 1/2	13790	6.7	66.4	2.8	E,F,G,H,I,J,K
567 1/4	4320	2.1	69.9	2.0	E,F,G,H,I,J,K
567	14900	7.2	54.9	9.1	E,F,G,H,I,J,K
566 3/4	1850	0.9	68.6	4.6	E,G,I,J
566 1/2	5190	2.5	53.6	3.2	E,G,I,J
566 1/4	1020	0.5	56.9	1.5	E,G,J,
566	5470	2.6	52.7	4.4	E,J
565 3/4	870	0.4	60.3	0.0	J
565 1/2	2110	1.0	55.5	8.3	J
565 1/4	1760	0.9	59.9	2.6	J
565	2320	1.1	52.8	9.1	J
564 3/4	290	0.1	58.6	3.4	J
564 1/2	2150	1.0	67.7	2.8	J
564 1/4	610	0.3	68.0	5.7	J
564	3490	1.7	55.4	13.2	J
563 3/4	60	0.0	50.0	0.0	J
563 1/2	120	0.1	33.3	0.0	J
	148,130	71.7	59.5	5.9	D,E,F,G,H,I,J,K

%Range   564
Daily   to
Volume   573

			% of Total	
			CTI1	CTI2
Total Volume For Nov 85 Soybeans	206.650		61.5	5.6
Total Volume for Soybeans	314,090		60.7	7.3
Total Spread Volume for Nov 85 Soybeans	11,390		52.2	4.0

7-16 Value area: 564-573
        Initiative 1) Selling at top, buying at bottom
        Initiative 2) Downside range extension
                 3) TPO count indicates even buying and selling

Trade Price	% of Volume	Total	CTI1%	CTI2%	Half Hour Bracket Times At Which Prices Occurred
573	1540	0.7	59.1	4.9	D
572 3/4	950	0.4	94.2	0.0	D
572 1/2	6630	3.1	38.2	5.6	D
572 1/4	930	0.4	93.5	5.9	D
572	2940	1.4	60.2	11.1	D
571 3/4	880	0.4	50.6	21.6	D
571 1/2	1750	0.8	60.6	11.7	D
571 1/4	270	0.1	74.1	9.3	D
571	2240	1.1	79.7	4.9	D
570 3/4	2710	1.3	67.2	3.1	D
570 1/2	6550	3.1	51.8	1.5	D
570 1/4	1170	0.6	80.3	0.0	D
570	9300	4.4	75.4	9.7	D
569 3/4	180	0.1	61.1	0.0	D
569 1/2	460	0.2	76.1	4.3	D
569 1/4	20	0.0	50.0	0.0	D
569	590	0.3	55.9	8.5	D,E
568 3/4	10150	4.8	0.6	44.4	D,E
568 1/2	2400	1.1	69.8	1.0	D,E
568 1/4	710	0.3	56.3	7.0	D,E
568	6510	3.1	54.6	19.4	D,E,K
567 3/4	3330	1.6	57.5	11.4	D,E,K
567 1/2	10930	5.2	63.5	7.2	D,E,F,J,K
567 1/4	4750	2.2	68.1	8.1	D,E,F,J,K
567	10640	5.0	64.2	10.6	D,E,F,J,K
566 3/4	2840	1.3	72.7	2.1	D,E,F,J,K
566 1/2	6680	3.2	56.7	3.1	D,E,F,J,K
566 1/4	4300	2.0	65.2	5.0	D,E,F,J,K
566	9460	4.5	62.6	9.6	D,E,F,J,K
565 3/4	5290	2.5	68.5	1.9	D,E,F,H,J,K
565 1/2	11160	5.3	56.6	7.3	D,E,F,H,J,K
565 1/4	3180	1.5	59.9	3.6	F,H,I,J,K
565	10820	5.1	61.3	15.9	F,H,J,K
564 3/4	3300	1.6	68.5	2.1	F,H,I,J,K
564 1/2	6820	3.2	76.2	2.3	F,H,I,J,K
564 1/4	3220	1.5	73.1	1.1	F,G,H,I,J
564	11150	5.3	65.2	5.8	F,G,H,I,J
563 3/4	4420	2.1	70.8	5.8	F,G,H,I,J
563 1/2	3760	1.8	58.2	6.6	F,G,H,I,J
563 1/4	2250	1.1	57.6	5.1	F,G,I,J
563	9420	4.4	57.7	3.1	F,G,I,J
562 3/4	1740	0.8	65.5	0.6	F,G,I,J
562 1/2	6780	3.2	55.3	2.9	F,I,J
562 1/4	1720	0.8	59.6	3.5	F,I,J
562	6040	2.8	55.5	5.8	F,I,J
561 3/4	1500	0.7	61.0	6.0	F,I,J
561 1/2	2990	1.4	54.6	20.6	F,I,J
561 1/4	540	0.3	66.7	1.9	I,J
561	2790	1.3	50.4	7.0	I,J
560 3/4	350	0.2	61.4	5.7	I
560 1/2	960	0.5	30.7	20.3	I
	150510	71.0	62.4	7.0	D,E,F,G,H,I,J,K

```
70 % Range      562
of Daily        to
Volume          568
                                                     % of Total
                                                   CTI1      CTI2

Total Volume for Nov 85 Soybeans     212,010      59.1       8.8
Total Volume for Soybeans            320,870      58.8       9.8
Total Spread Volume for Nov 85 Soybeans  15,255  78.3       9.0

7-17 Value area 562-568
                    1) Selling at top (initiating),
                       buying at bottom (responsive)
         Initiative 2) Downside range extension
         Responsive 3) TPO count indicates buying
```

Trade Price	% of Volume	Total	CTI1%	CTI2%	Half Hour Bracket Times At Which Prices Occurred
565 1/2	1510	0.9	56.0	0.0	D
565 1/4	70	0.0	85.7	0.0	D
565	3820	2.2	58.9	13.0	D
564 3/4	590	0.3	55.9	0.8	D
564 1/2	2880	1.7	66.3	2.4	D
564 1/4	800	0.5	70.0	0.0	D
564	5270	3.1	70.1	6.8	D
563 3/4	3260	1.9	52.1	28.2	D,J
563 1/2	5140	3.0	51.6	14.0	D,J
563 1/4	1150	0.7	67.0	0.4	D,J
563	9490	5.5	55.7	10.4	D,J
562 3/4	1510	0.9	61.3	1.7	D,J
562 1/2	13650	8.0	41.7	21.0	D,E,H,I,J,K
562 1/4	2700	1.6	66.3	3.7	D,E,H,I,J,K
562	17210	10.1	59.1	7.1	D,E,F,G,H,I,K
561 3/4	4740	2.8	63.3	5.1	D,E,F,G,H,I,K
561 1/2	13080	7.6	66.1	8.8	D,E,F,G,H,I,K
561 1/4	3840	2.2	66.9	2.5	D,E,F,G,H,I,K
561	15750	9.2	61.0	7.0	D,E,F,G,H,I,K
560 3/4	3930	2.3	66.9	2.5	D,E,F,G,H,I,K
560 1/2	10970	6.4	60.4	9.1	D,E,F,G,H,I,K
560 1/4	1690	1.0	67.5	2.4	E.G,H,I
560	6170	3.6	61.8	14.7	E,G,H,I
559 3/4	1660	1.0	65.7	3.3	E,G,H
559 1/2	3600	2.1	61.3	8.5	E,G,H
559 1/4	1420	0.8	57.7	20.4	E,G,H
559	10200	6.0	58.5	16.5	E,G,H
558 3/4	1720	1.0	59.3	22.7	E,G,H
558 1/2	7310	4.3	58.9	10.0	E,G,H
558 1/4	2710	1.6	53.9	11.8	E,H
558	8790	5.1	59.3	17.2	E,H
557 3/4	140	0.1	57.1	0.0	E
557 1/2	2860	1.7	60.8	6.1	E
557 1/4	240	0.1	43.8	27.1	E
557	1240	0.7	25.8	25.8	E
	121210	70.8	59.2	9.8	D,E,F,G,H,I,J,K

70 % Range of Daily Volume	559 3/4 to 564

		% of Total CTI1	CTI2
Total Volume for Nov 85 Soybeans	171110	59.0	10.7
Total Volume for Soybeans	247970	57.6	11.3
Total Spread Volume for Nov 85 Soybeans	8715	54.8	23.6

7-18 Value area 559 3/4-564
        Responsive 1) Selling at top, buying at bottom
                   2) No range extension
        Responsive 3) TPO count indicates buying

Trade Price	% of Volume	Total	CTI1%	CTI2%	Half Hour Bracket Times At Which Prices Occurred
555 3/4	380	0.3	55.3	3.9	E
555 1/2	2010	1.4	56.7	23.9	E
555 1/4	510	0.4	66.7	1.0	E
555	3950	2.8	63.9	10.4	D,E
554 3/4	710	0.5	62.0	2.8	D,E
554 1/2	3670	2.6	65.7	4.8	D,E,F
554 1/4	2690	1.9	76.4	6.5	D,E,F
554	10630	7.5	58.6	9.0	D,E,F,G,H
553 3/4	3840	2.7	73.6	6.5	D,E,F,G,H
553 1/2	12610	8.9	60.5	9.0	D,E,F,G,H,K
553 1/4	6990	4.9	64.1	12.2	D,E,F,G,H,I,K
553	30120	21.3	51.1	16.3	D,E,F,G,H,I,K
552 3/4	3950	2.8	62.7	8.1	D,F,H,I,J,K
552 1/2	14520	10.3	53.7	11.6	D,F,I,J,K
552 1/4	4820	3.4	65.2	1.8	D,F,I,J,K
552	16500	11.7	52.5	6.5	D,I,J,K
551 3/4	2480	1.8	69.2	3.6	D,J,K
551 1/2	4800	3.4	49.4	3.6	D,J,K
551 1/4	2690	1.9	51.9	0.7	D,J,K
551	10650	7.5	47.3	16.9	D,J,K
550 3/4	1520	1.1	75.3	3.9	J
550 1/2	1340	0.9	60.8	12.7	J
	103980	73.5	56.4	10.8	D,E,F,G,H,I,J,K

70% Range	552				
of Daily	to				
Volume	554				% of Total
					CTI1 CTI2

		% of Total	
		CTI1	CTI2
Total Volume for Nov 85 Soybeans	141380	56.8	10.5
Total Volume for Soybeans	222910	56.1	10.1
Total Spread Volume for Nov 85 Soybeans	10800	43.5	14.5

7-19 Value area 552-554
                1) Selling on top, (initiative),
                  buying at bottom (responsive)
     Initiative 2) Downside range extension
                3) TPO count indicates even buying and selling

Trade Price	% of Volume	Total	CTI1%	CTI2%	Half Hour Bracket Times At Which Prices Occurred
556 3/4	390	0.3	51.3	23.1	K
556 1/2	1730	1.2	54.6	0.6	J,K
556 1/4	930	0.7	63.4	0.0	J,K
556	3150	2.3	64.1	6.8	J,K
555 3/4	1520	1.1	68.8	2.6	J,K
555 1/2	2720	2.0	78.1	2.0	J,K
555 1/4	1290	0.9	64.7	0.0	H,J,K
555	3330	2.4	58.1	9.8	H,J,K
554 3/4	1650	1.2	62.4	7.3	H,J,K
554 1/2	3040	2.2	67.1	4.9	H,J,K
554 1/4	1880	1.4	58.8	9.8	G,H,J,K
554	8060	5.8	66.4	9.2	G,H,I,J,K
553 3/4	5200	3.7	77.6	1.2	F,G,H,I,J,K
553 1/2	7380	5.3	67.5	6.4	E,F,G,H,I,J,K
553 1/4	3150	2.3	75.7	3.0	E,F,G,H,I,J
553	7060	5.1	73.1	3.4	E,F,G,H,I,J
552 3/4	4950	3.6	66.5	3.0	E,F,G,H,I,J
552 1/2	6070	4.4	61.7	5.5	D,E,F,G,H,I,J
552 1/4	3220	2.3	69.7	6.4	D,E,F,G,H,I,J
552	9090	6.5	58.9	11.9	D,E,F,G,I,J
551 3/4	1650	1.2	65.8	0.3	D,E,F,I,J
551 1/2	4520	3.3	54.9	17.3	D,E,I,J
551 1/4	960	0.7	53.6	1.0	D,E,I,J
551	5220	3.8	67.5	5.3	D,E,J
550 3/4	3920	2.8	68.2	5.9	D,E,J
550 1/2	5950	4.3	63.4	5.5	D,E,J
550 1/4	3110	2.2	73.2	3.1	D,E
550	24120	17.4	52.8	9.8	D,E
549 3/4	3260	2.3	71.3	2.0	D,E
549 1/2	5960	4.3	71.8	3.4	D
549 1/4	1690	1.2	60.4	6.2	D
549	2760	2.0	49.8	7.6	D
548 3/4	80	0.1	56.3	0.0	D

70% Range of Daily Volume	549 1/2 to 553 1/2			% of Total

7-22 Value area 549 1/2-553 1/2
        Responsive 1) Buying at bottom
        Initiative 2) Upside range extension
        Responsive 3) TPO indicates selling

Trade Price	% of Volume	Total	CTI1%	CTI2%	Half Hour Bracket Times At Which Prices Occurred
558 1/2	110	0.1	100.0	0.0	D
558 1/4	30	0.0	50.0	0.0	D
558	5000	2.5	57.1	7.8	D
557 3/4	700	0.4	70.7	5.7	D
557 1/2	4620	2.3	63.2	3.5	D
557 1/4	740	0.4	61.5	13.5	D
557	9640	4.9	57.7	4.8	D,E
556 3/4	1870	0.9	66.0	5.3	D,E
556 1/2	4850	2.4	72.0	1.3	D,E
556 1/4	2810	1.4	66.5	6.2	D,E,F
556	13730	6.9	61.2	14.7	D,E,F
555 3/4	3250	1.6	71.7	2.8	D,E,F
555 1/2	5220	2.6	51.1	6.8	D,E,F
555 1/4	3290	1.7	71.8	1.1	D,E,F,G
555	6950	3.5	66.2	8.6	D,E,F,G
554 3/4	1490	0.8	57.0	4.7	D,F,G
554 1/2	3870	2.0	64.6	1.3	D,F,G
554 1/4	1720	0.9	69.2	6.4	D,G
554	4920	2.5	64.0	11.9	D,G
553 3/4	730	0.4	43.2	30.1	D,G
553 1/2	1910	1.0	41.4	1.3	G,H
553 1/4	1100	0.6	55.9	1.8	G,H
553	4050	2.0	51.4	4.7	G,H
552 3/4	3130	1.6	62.6	4.5	G,H
552 1/2	4740	2.4	58.5	5.1	G,H
552 1/4	2070	1.0	66.9	11.1	G,H,I
552	4870	2.5	50.7	6.9	G,H,I
551 3/4	1050	0.5	74.8	2.9	G,H,I
551 1/2	2390	1.7	59.6	8.1	H,I
551 1/4	1250	0.6	54.4	7.2	H,I
551	4340	2.2	60.0	5.1	H,I
550 3/4	970	0.5	72.7	0.0	H,I
550 1/2	1110	0.6	36.5	9.0	H,I
550 1/4	1410	0.7	52.5	5.0	I
550	7050	3.6	51.6	4.5	I
549 3/4	530	0.3	38.7	1.9	I
549 1/2	310	0.2	75.8	0.0	I
549 1/4	110	0.1	50.0	22.7	I
549	1250	0.6	58.8	2.8	I,J
548 3/4	1700	0.9	50.0	13.5	I,J
548 1/2	3680	1.9	55.3	11.7	I,J
548 1/4	1970	1.0	62.9	3.6	I,J
548	6040	3.5	55.2	12.3	I,J
547 3/4	2430	1.2	62.1	9.3	I,J
547 1/2	3090	1.6	65.4	0.3	I,J
547 1/4	1960	1.0	63.5	3.1	I,J
547	5480	2.8	58.9	15.0	J
546 3/4	1600	0.8	68.8	5.6	J
546 1/2	2240	1.1	58.3	17.2	J
546 1/4	1410	0.7	61.7	6.0	J
546	2960	1.5	46.6	25.8	J,K
545 3/4	1270	0.6	74.0	4.3	J,K
545 1/2	3930	2.0	49.6	18.4	J,K
545 1/4	1740	0.9	69.3	2.9	J,K
545	6690	3.4	49.6	17.4	K
544 3/4	540	0.3	57.4	0.9	K
544 1/2	1040	0.5	53.4	0.0	K
544 1/4	270	0.1	38.9	0.0	K
544	2010	1.0	46.0	16.9	K
543 3/4	450	0.2	53.3	0.0	K
543 1/2	1880	0.9	53.2	0.0	K
543 1/4	20	0.0	25.0	0.0	K
543	3570	1.8	58.3	14.8	K
542 3/4	110	0.1	63.6	0.0	K
542 1/2	1790	0.9	65.4	1.4	K
542 1/4	NA				
542	4260	2.2	48.1	14.0	K
541 3/4	30	0.0	16.7	0.0	K
541 1/2	2460	1.2	56.7	13.0	K
541 1/4	510	0.3	65.7	18.6	K
541	7590	3.8	52.6	8.1	K
540 3/4	130	0.1	92.3	0.0	K
540 1/2	1700	0.9	63.2	8.2	K
540 1/4	40	0.0	50.0	0.0	K
540	510	0.3	50.0	0.0	K
	139740	70.6	59.8	7.0	D,E,F,G,H,I,J

70% Range of Daily Volume	547 1/2 to 558			

			% of Total	
			CTI1	CTI2
Total Volume for Nov 85 Soybeans	198070		58.5	8.4
Total Volume for Soybeans	284560		58.5	7.8
Total Spread Volume for Nov 85 Soybeans	11140		53.9	7.1

7-23 Value area 547 1/2-558
    Responsive 1) Selling at top
      Initiative 2) Downside range extension (Responsive to Initiative)
      Initiative 3) TPO count indicates selling

Trade Price	% of Volume	Total	CTI1%	CTI2%	Half Hour Bracket Times At Which Prices Occurred
543 1/2	2640	1.5	56.1	8.5	D,E
543 1/4	1080	0.6	61.6	0.9	D,E
543	5240	2.9	63.5	12.6	D.E
542 3/4	3830	2.1	67.6	7.8	D,E
542 1/2	7830	4.3	55.6	10.5	D,E
542 1/4	2050	1.1	68.8	5.1	D,E
542	13710	7.6	59.7	12.2	D,E,F
541 3/4	6090	3.4	67.7	8.3	D,E,F
541 1/2	6240	3.5	66.7	9.8	D,E,F
541 1/4	720	0.4	82.6	2.8	D,F
541	5770	3.2	52.4	23.5	D,F
540 3/4	750	0.4	57.3	9.3	D,F
540 1/2	2820	1.6	58.9	5.1	D,F
540 1/4	1450	0.8	64.5	0.7	D,F
540	23700	13.2	61.7	11.7	D,F,G
539 3/4	750	0.4	71.3	1.3	D.F,G,H
539 1/2	4710	2.6	56.8	12.1	D,F,G,H
539 1/4	2570	1.4	70.0	4.5	F,G,H,I
539	9680	5.4	52.5	17.7	F,G,H,I
538 3/4	6830	3.8	60.7	12.4	F,G,H,I
538 1/2	4800	2.7	63.1	7.7	F,G,H,I,J,K
538 1/4	5410	3.0	64.3	4.3	F,G,H,I,J,K
538	15180	8.4	55.3	10.2	F,G,I,J,K
537 3/4	4020	2.2	68.5	5.8	F,G,I,J,K
537 1/2	8400	4.7	58.3	9.4	F,I,J,K
537 1/4	3860	2.1	63.7	6.1	F,I,J,K
537	12120	6.7	53.3	10.1	I,J,K
536 3/4	4500	2.5	76.6	3.0	I,J,K
536 1/2	6530	3.6	55.5	8.3	I,J,K
536 1/4	2100	1.2	63.3	7.1	I,J,K
536	3770	2.1	59.4	14.3	I,J,K
535 3/4	180	0.1	61.1	2.8	K
535 1/2	870	0.5	16.1	0.0	K
	129720	72.0	59.4	10.5	D,F,G,H,I,J,K

70% Range of Daily Volume	536 to 541			
			% of Total	
		CTI1	CTI2	
Total Volume for Nov 85 Soybeans	180200	60.0	10.3	
Total Volume for Soybeans	270180	59.3	9.5	
Total Spread Volume for Nov 85 Soybeans	11220	46.3	24.5	

7-24 Value area 536-541
           1) Buying on Bottom
Initiative 2) Downside range extension
Initiative 3) TPO count indicates selling

Trade Price	% of Volume	Total	CTI1%	CTI2%	Half Hour Bracket Times At Which Prices Occurred
541 3/4	60	0.0	25.0	16.7	G
541 1/2	2870	1.9	61.8	8.2	F,G,H
541 1/4	1480	1.0	67.9	0.7	F,G,H,I
541	4940	3.3	70.4	7.2	F,G,H,I,K
540 3/4	2500	1.6	69.4	5.6	F,G,H,I,K
540 1/2	7290	4.8	65.6	2.2	F,G,H,I,J,K
540 1/4	4060	2.7	69.6	1.5	F,G,H,I,J,K
540	14260	9.4	64.0	11.7	D,F,G,H,I,J,K
539 3/4	4760	3.1	73.3	5.0	D,F,G,H,I,J,K
539 1/2	13000	8.6	64.9	5.8	D,F,G,H,I,J,K
539 1/4	5770	3.8	78.9	4.8	D,F,G,H,I,J,K
539	12290	8.1	61.4	9.8	D,E,F,G,H,I,J,K
538 3/4	1880	1.2	66.5	4.5	D,E,F,G,H,J
538 1/2	4710	3.1	72.7	12.4	D,E,F,G,H,J
538 1/4	2870	1.9	74.4	2.1	D,E,F
538	21910	14.4	73.9	3.8	D,E,F
537 3/4	4410	2.9	82.9	5.6	D,E,F
537 1/2	9020	5.9	70.6	3.9	D,E,F
537 1/4	2680	1.8	74.1	5.8	D,E,F
537	8300	5.5	69.8	8.0	D,E
536 3/4	1880	1.2	60.4	1.9	D,E
536 1/2	4540	3.0	50.3	2.8	D,E
536 1/4	200	0.1	47.5	0.0	D
536	8980	5.9	41.6	19.5	D
535 3/4	680	0.4	55.1	15.4	D
535 1/2	1740	1.1	62.9	7.5	D
535 1/4	1240	0.8	73.0	0.4	D
535	2630	1.7	58.7	2.1	D
534 3/4	710	0.5	24.6	28.2	D
534 1/2	230	0.2	41.3	0.0	D
	109920	72.4	69.8	6.5	D,E,F,G,H,I,J,K

70% Range   537
of Daily   to
Volume   540 1/4

		% of Total	
		CTI1	CTI2
Total Volume for Nov 85 Soybeans	151890	66.5	6.9
Total Volume for Soybeans	231140	62.5	9.9
Total Spread Volume for Nov 85 Soybeans	9030	45.2	23.3

7-25 Value area:537-540 1/4
        Initiative 1) Buying at bottom
        Initiative 2) Upside range extension
        Responsive 3) TPO count indicates selling

Trade Price	% of Volume	Total	CTI1%	CTI2%	Half Hour Bracket Times At Which Prices Occurred
545	1000	0.8	21.0	10.5	I
544 3/4	390	0.3	74.4	1.3	I
544 1/2	2290	1.7	55.7	8.7	I,J
544 1/4	3260	2.5	56.3	14.9	I,J
544	7190	5.4	58.1	9.9	I,J
543 3/4	3340	2.5	75.1	11.8	I,J
543 1/2	4020	3.0	53.5	17.7	I,J
543 1/4	1810	1.4	60.5	0.8	I,J
543	5510	4.2	62.7	8.4	I,J,K
542 3/4	2400	1.8	66.9	6.5	I,J,K
542 1/2	4720	3.6	57.1	10.8	I,J,K
542 1/4	650	0.5	76.9	1.5	I,J,K
542	3830	2.9	42.6	24.2	D,E,H,I,K
541 3/4	2790	2.1	68.3	3.0	D,E,H,I,K
541 1/2	4560	3.4	66.2	6.6	D,E,H,I,K
541 1/4	2110	1.6	61.8	5.0	D,E,F,H,I,K
541	6020	4.5	63.5	16.0	D,E,F,G,H,K
540 3/4	5000	3.8	64.4	5.8	D,E,F,G,H,K
540 1/2	5300	4.0	61.0	7.0	D,E,F,G,H,K
540 1/4	3920	3.0	71.0	1.7	D,E,G,H,K
540	14340	10.8	64.7	8.4	D,E,G,H,K
539 3/4	2300	1.7	63.3	8.3	D,G,H,K
539 1/2	7040	5.3	62.5	1.8	D,H,K
539 1/4	3340	2.5	66.6	3.1	D,H,K
539	10330	7.8	68.7	6.3	D,K
538 3/4	930	0.7	71.5	4.3	D,K
538 1/3	4700	3.6	63.5	11.2	D,K
538 1/4	430	0.3	55.8	7.0	D,K
538	5010	3.8	51.9	13.2	K
537 3/4	420	0.3	75.0	0.0	K
537 1/2	2310	1.7	55.4	13.2	K
537 1/4	150	0.1	60.0	0.0	K
537	3310	2.5	49.2	11.8	K
536 3/4	290	0.2	82.8	0.0	K
536 1/2	4800	3.6	46.7	11.0	K
536 1/4	350	0.3	82.9	0.0	K
536	2170	1.6	59.4	12.9	K
	95230	72.0	63.1	8.2	D,E,F,G,H,I,J,K

70% Range of Daily Volume	538 to 543		

		% of Total	
		CTI1	CTI2
Total Volume for Nov 85 Soybeans	132330	61.2	9.0
Total Volume for Soybeans	191370	59.9	9.8
Total Spread Volume for Nov 85 Soybeans	9365	62.3	6.8

7-26 Value area: 538-543
               1) Selling at top
    Initiative 2) Upside range extension
  Responsive 3) TPO count indicates selling

Step 2 -- Running Commentary

This running commentary on soybeans will interpret how the market is establishing value and what the level of activity of the other timeframe buyers and sellers reveals about the market.

On the first day, the soybean market is neutral, indicating very little activity of other timeframe traders. This shows day timeframe traders eliciting a fair price area so that trade can take place. Once that area is found, the market will remain there unless influenced by the entrance of the other timeframe trader, the participant who has the ability to change a market's structure. Note that the value area has a narrow range. This narrowness indicates that this area was not facilitating trade. Thus, the market cannot stay in this condition for long, and one should note that any activity changing the market should be classified as initiating activity.

Early in the second day, trade begins at about the same level of the first day's value area. Once below this area, the market moves lower quickly. Other timeframe sellers are active at the top of the range, and cause range extension to the downside. The time-price opportunity (TPO) count is even, indicating that other timeframe buying and selling was even in the value area. Other timeframe buying occurred at the bottom of the range in response to the opportunity. The TPO count being even, after the initial wave of selling, day timeframe traders had to find support in the market in order to have two-sided trade. The sharp market movement went low enough to first stop the impetus of selling and in fact found some responsive buying that served as early support, and later was equalized when the selling returned. The wide range in value area shows that the market was facilitating trade, and that selling definitely was the initiating activity. Selling was expected to be slowed but has not ended.

On the third day, the market had slightly lower to unchanged values. Selling activity was indicated at the top of the range in response to the higher prices. Further, range extension to the downside was initiating activity. The TPO count indicated responsive buying by the other timeframe buyer in the value area and again at the bottom of the range. Note that other timeframe sellers stayed in an initiating mode with buyers only in a responding mode.

The fourth day, lower values follow with responsive buying at the bottom. The TPO count indicates buying in the value area, but with responsive selling above the previous day's value area. Note that there is no range extension, so that initiating action is absent on this day, but the down auction remains. Other timeframe traders wish to become responsive sellers rather than initiating sellers. Given an opportunity, sellers will still be apparent.

On the fifth day, the market opened sharply lower due to a dominant concern over some weather or news related influence. The market showed some initiating selling at the top of the range, a range extension to the downside that failed, and a TPO count in the value area was even. The value area was extremely narrow, illustrating that the market was not facilitating trade at this new level, and that the sharp price break had brought about some — but little — activity from the other timeframe seller. The failure to extend the range gives the day timeframe traders — as well as other timeframe buyers — confidence to begin some buying activity. In other words, the other timeframe buyer needs to surface in order for the market to read his activity and the fact that he did not show much activity is an indication of his passivity. Thus, the market is coming down to lower levels, thereby offering more attractive opportunities for the other timeframe buyer. Yet he is not at this time taking advantage of them, and we can assume he will not unless forced to change. Sellers, on the other hand, having temporarily removed their anxiety, at present want to take advantage or respond to market-created opportunities.

During the sixth day, there was an attempt to initiate buying activity when the market opened below the previous day's value area, and then went back up through these values as other timeframe buyers responded to the early low prices. Their level of activity was high; they initiated by extending the range upward. This was their first initiating activity in the sample, and was met with the expected selling by other timeframe traders in response to the opportunity. Note that the lack of early selling brought about buying which in turn continued until the selling response was found.

The seventh day sees the other timeframe sellers respond to a market-created opportunity by selling aggressively at the top of the range. They are initiating activity in the value area causing range extension, and dominating activity in the value area, producing net TPO selling as indicated in the count. That other timeframe sellers are still present and dominant at lower price levels indicates that the down auction is still intact, since trade is being facilitated the lower the market moves.

On the eighth day, downside range extension shows sellers initiating activity, and the TPO count also indicates net selling. The extremes, however, showed no other timeframe activity. The narrow value areas show that volume is being handled by the day timeframe trader and that the other timeframe trader is not very active.

On the ninth day, the market has relatively unchanged values, with initiating buying at the bottom and range extension to the upside that is met with responsive TPO selling. On the last day of the sample, the market shows initial initiating buying at the bottom of the range (remove the G through K against D period) and a range extension to the upside with relatively unchanged values and TPO selling in response. There also was responsive selling at the top of the range in response to range extension by the initiating other timeframe buyers. The buying then becomes passive, as selling initiated a further range extension to the downside late in the day. Usually a double range extension indicates that the day will be a neutral day. Neutral days revert to the original auction direction. This is an example of a split day or a day split into two parts. It points out that while at the same prices other timeframe buyers and sellers fail to come together, they can use the same prices at different times during the day.

The whole sample shows a down auction with little aggressiveness on the part of the other timeframe buyer. He really only surfaced responsively or when he was the only other timeframe participant. The other timeframe seller was being forced by this situation to continue his activity throughout the range of our sample. He took advantage of the situation offered as best he could and was by far the most aggressive in setting the tone of the auction. His continued presence at this lower level means that the market has not gone low enough to shut off the activity in this large auction sequence. The down auction will continue so long as his behavior and activity level continue.

Step 3 -- "Free Exposure"

When an individual seeking free exposure uses the data as a decision support tool, he can deduce as the second day unfolds that the market is in a down auction. The value areas of the second day were never breached nor was there an absence of other timeframe seller activity. He initiated and responded in far greater fashion than the other timeframe buyer. It needs to be understood that the sellers do not like to follow and continuously sell as the market goes lower, nor do buyers like to continually buy higher. Thus, if this activity is demonstrated you can deduce that this behavior is being forced, rather than voluntary.

Remember that the participants we monitor are responding voluntarily or are being forced by their circumstance. You can see that sharply changed prices do cause activity to slow down, particularly on the fifth day, the 19th. The buyers waited until the lower prices on the sixth day, the 22nd, were rejected and the values of the previous day were violated until they responded. This means that the long-term buyer was given every opportunity to continue to respond. Before he responded, he made sure that there was an absence of other timeframe sellers before committing. In other words, the lack of range extension (failed on the fifth day), the lack of selling in the TPO area in the face of little buying, were information sources that motivated the long timeframe buyer. The other timeframe buyer's readings motivated his activities. Although we attribute this as initiating activity, it was in actuality more of a forced response due to the exhausted activity of the seller.

With the initiating and response activity of the other timeframe seller, one could take a short position in almost any instance except for the fifth day and early the sixth day. A set of circumstances on the 19th and early 22nd (fifth, sixth) were the only set of circumstance wherein one could launch a free exposure long position. Throughout this sample, values moved lower, and when selling activity slowed, only unchanged values developed, i.e., the other timeframe buyers only accepted these lower values and never upset this balance of the market. This is a clear down auction which will continue. The activity levels in the last few days of this sample.

As a point of conclusion, when looking for a "free exposure" situation, look for initiating activity throughout the range, whether in an up or down main auction. Look for responsive action in all three categories when one is with the major action direction. Logically, one is able to take this position because in order to stop this activity, the market will have to continue to move directionally in order to shut it off.

III. Practical Applications for the Investor-Trader

11

HOW BEST TO GET RESULTS

T he vast majority of participants in exchange marketplaces lose
because they do not examine, ponder and try to improve what
can be termed their overall approach to the market. An approach
would be a framework encompassing all the variables which combine
to collectively spell either success or failure in a marketplace. In
principle, an individual seeking success in the automobile market
would employ the same approach as he would in the housing market,
in futures, stocks, any market in existence or virtually any endeavor.
Thus, defining and then examining one's approach is as important a
step for a marketing executive responsible for pricing decisions as it is
for a futures or stock trader. Yet very few participants have ever even
defined for themselves the equation for investing and trading results
which would specify or enumerate all the key components or variables
which will account for their success or failure. Thus, few participants
have an organized framework from which to monitor those variables,
adjust for patterns, and begin improving their trading results.

The Equation for Results and the Two Possible Approaches

Our equation for trading or investing results which enumerates the
components of one's overall approach given a specific opportunity is:

Your market understanding x (you + your trading strategy) = results.

Consideration of this equation reveals two alternative market
approaches: one assumes randomness in market behavior and market

efficiency, and therefore does not see the possibility of developing a market understanding, since the behavior of a random object cannot be understood in terms of cause and effect. The second approach assumes the market cannot be random but acts due to cause and effect, and thus places great emphasis on developing an understanding of the market and its conditions in order to isolate the motivating causes. The first approach makes success much more difficult by relying on the strength of the individual to overcome a lack of information sufficient for logical decision making. The second makes success more readily available for the average person, since decision making relies on a sound market understanding based on presently available information, thus reducing the pressure on the individual to make decisions with confidence and poise while uninformed. The first approach unknowingly forces the individual to rely on his strength as an individual, and to act in ways and under situations that few humans can. The second approach allows him to capitalize on his personal decision making strengths while acknowledging and minimizing his weaknesses. The first is the current approach embraced by the academic community and the second is the logical approach advocated by the authors in this book.

Given an identical (you + your trading strategy), the determinant for each individual's success level revolves around the difference in market understanding — the ability to correctly read and interpret the market's up-to-the-minute condition so as to accurately deduce when exceptional trading opportunity exists. Yet because of their lack of awareness of the principles espoused in this book, a complete or near complete lack of market understanding is exactly what most participants face. Given the above equation, consider the rather drastic disadvantage one faces when approaching a market with no (zero) market understanding.

To overcome a lack of information from which to generate decisions, most traders and investors resort to attempting to predict the market's future direction, forfeiting a market understanding. This approach to a marketplace unknowingly accepts a 50% probability factor, since in a market of uncertainty any systematic predictive approach is going to be right 50% of the time and wrong 50% of the time, when applied consistently over a statistically large sample size.

When the average trader or investor begins by trying to forecast the market's direction, he protects himself from his lack of market understanding with a defensive trading strategy. Such a defensive strategy includes entering the market only with a predetermined profit and (especially) loss point, the latter being known in organized markets as a stop-loss order. While for the average person, predicting might do little better than 50-50, when accompanied by the use of stops, the percentage of positions based on predictions are going to be correct no

better than 50% of the time. Consider that on any purchase there are
but three possible outcomes over the immediate or short timeframe:

1. **The market moves up.**
2. **The market doesn't move up but it doesn't break.**
3. **The market breaks.**

For example, the key to success on a series of purchases (long
position) is not only to have the first outcome, but merely to avoid the
third outcome. Most individuals who lack a market understanding do
not know why the second outcome is acceptable, and under what
conditions it is preferred.

While defensive, the use of stop orders is not over the long term a
successful or winning strategy. To illustrate why, assume that the
buyer enters the market and uses a "sell-stop" loss point which may
on occasion be triggered by outcome #2 and will be triggered by
outcome #3. By employing the defensive use of stops, he is thus
willing to take either #1 or #3, whichever comes first. He is not
affected by the #2 outcome, since his parameters are outside the
consideration of price standing still through time. By using stops, the
trader is thus willing to accept one event happening before another in
a market of uncertainty, a strategy which is at most a 50-50 proposition
over a large sample size.

Over a large sample size, the scenario #2 occurs regularly, and the
individual who has a market understanding and does not use price
stop-loss points gains an advantage of 1% to 16%, depending on the
frequency of all three events. If we can assume that each of the three
scenarios occurs equally, then by halting the use of a stop-loss, the
participant with a market understanding has a 66% chance of not losing
any capital. Indeed, he has the same percentage for success as the
individual who predicts and uses stops, but by improving his loss
percentage — decreasing the percentage of losing trades — he dramatically improves his odds for success over the long term.

Thus, by discarding the stop-loss order strategy, one gains a
substantial percentage advantage over the user of stop-loss orders.
Furthermore, logic dictates that using a stop-loss order predicated
solely on price parameters assumes that all prices have the same
significance, an assumption the participant with a market understanding knows to be false. The market manages itself through time
and promotes itself through price, so the trader who manages his
trading decisions solely on price is out of step with market reality.

Yet, users of stops often lose in other ways. If the market moves in
the desired direction, the individual with a market understanding,
sensing the market's strong condition, may profit much more substantially than the individual with a predetermined and inflexible profit

point. And as the market moves against both, the individual with the market understanding will monitor the market and act accordingly. Understanding the condition of the market, he can be comfortable watching price move against him, secure in his knowledge that the structure of the market never changes instantaneously and that he has time to exit the position. He gets concerned only when the market's structure warrants. [5] In contrast, the trader who uses stop-loss orders and profit objectives faces the dilemma of how much loss is acceptable. If the stop is placed too close, he may watch the market move against him just far enough to hit his stop and then quickly rally back in his direction without his participation. If the stop is placed too far, he will not exit the trade prior to losing substantial capital.

Thus, in a market of uncertainty, an approach which is willing to take whichever comes first, a profit or loss (in other words, one which does not manage for the current situation), yields a 50% probability of success over a large sample size, given no (zero) execution costs and a 100% effective "you" and "trading strategy." The problem is that execution costs exist and that no human is capable of 100% efficiency all the time; humans respond to unobjective, illogical factors. So, if one were to allow for human frailty, and assume a 70% "you effectiveness," the equation would yield only a 35% probability of success. This simplistic discussion should illustrate that most average people have to overcome at least 15% deficiency in order to break even (not to mention commissions) in an organized market.

This is not to say that success cannot be or has not been achieved on a consistent basis by predicting and without the benefits of a logical market understanding. But it is rather unlikely for all but a very few traders to regularly achieve successful results with such an approach. The vast majority cannot be consistently accurate forecasters. And their approach keeps most traders and investors from developing a market understanding.

On the other hand, given the fact that a person should and can have a 100% understanding of what is going on in the present tense – not that this high level of understanding will always occur, but assuming the person will limit his trades to times when it does – a 100% up-to-the-moment market understanding is possible. The resulting percentage of success when allowing for the "you" will be dramatically higher, and all other things being equal, successful results will be more easily achieved. A 100% understanding will not occur all the time, but a market understanding of 80% x 70% effective you = 56% results factor. This is a dramatic increase in the odds for success when constant you and trading strategy is factored in. The market understanding approach puts the individual in a much more advantageous situation. It puts him in an environment in which a normal human being can ask himself to function comfortably, an environment which puts the percentages in his favor.

Before continuing to make a more in-depth comparison of the two market approaches — no market understanding versus a market understanding — consider the first approach, the current trading-investing approach, and its practical application for investors and traders.

The Current Approach to Trading

The current approach to trading does not rely on a sound, logical understanding and approach to the marketplace, in sharp contrast to the classical approach to investing espoused by Graham and Dodd in *Securities Analysis,* which clearly does. In the eyes of some, such a blanket statement may seem too strong, bordering on hyperbole. However, this statement is not so strong when one realizes that few market participants who consider themselves traders actually understand what it is they are doing. In other words, with the current trading approach, there is often a significant difference between what the trader thinks he is doing, and the reality of what he is actually doing. The current approach is such that many who believe they are trading are in fact investing, and vice versa. These statements may seem preposterous in light of the fact that most market participants are well educated, but problems exist because there are no generally understood definitions of trading and investing which have a basis in reality. [6]

To begin to discuss the current state of trading, definitions of investing and trading and hence the distinction between them need to be understood, so that the illogical deductions which contribute to misconceptions can be pinpointed.

Trading and Investing

Trading and investing are essentially identical. In both macro and micro sense, and in both theory and reality, they operate logically, relying on the same principles. Both have as goals the enhancement of capital with minimal capital exposure. There is no distinction between the two from a risk standpoint. Both may or may not involve leverage, and to differing degrees, and since neither is relegated to a specific market, neither is prima facie more or less risky than the other.

In both sound investing and sound trading, one seeks to enter a position where one is purchasing below value or selling above it, managing this position through time. This approach to investing was presented in the work, *Securities Analysis.* In it, Graham and Dodd assumed that the market was not efficient, and that value and price in the securities markets are two distinct things. At times the market will undervalue a security, and at other times it will overvalue it.

The work dealt with publicly held companies, entities which regularly reported performance information in the form of annual balance sheets which listed assets, income statements, quarterly sales and earnings reports, and other information which can be translated into per share profits and value. Graham and Dodd analyzed this information outside the marketplace in order to evaluate the earnings stream and asset value. They then compared their conclusions about the company's current value (taking into account such variables as risk-free rate, etc.) to the current market price of the stock. They then could ascertain if the organized market price was below, at or above their valuation. Any time a price is away from value, an opportunity exists.

Graham and Dodd's approach holds as true in other markets as it does in the securities markets: find something which is undervalued and buy it. Over time, assuming conditions remain unchanged, it will reach fair value and demand may increase to such an extent that it can be sold above value.

However, not all markets are as easily studied as the securities markets. In other words, futures markets and virtually all markets outside the realm of the equity world do not lend themselves to regular study of outside information which relates to either asset value or current earnings power. However, the importance of ascertaining value in markets which do not have an extensive information flow is identical to those that do. In other words, the job of differentiating between price and value may be more difficult in futures than in securities markets, yet its importance for success for the investor/trader is identical.

While both trading and investing have the same goal, they differ in two ways: the type of information used in the decision-making process and the management approach employed. As you will see, the type of information each focuses on determines their respective management approaches. [7]

Information

Both trader and investor use information to generate decisions and both have a sound basis for doing so. They differ in the type of information they place primary importance on when making a buy-sell decision. Investors place primary importance on information generated outside the marketplace: balance sheet, income statements, quarterly sales and earnings reports, the potential demand for an emerging technology or new product, management, favorable legislation, the overall investment and economic climate, etc. Investors relate this information to the marketplace in assessing probable change in value, either ignoring or placing as secondary in importance the market-generated information regarding changes in market value.

Traders also seek and apply outside information, but they place primary importance on information generated by the market itself. This information is analyzed within the context of specific opportunities, and the vast majority of trading decisions are based on it, possibly within a backdrop of information outside the market. Thus, the investor neither seeks information on nor heavily regards short-term market moves, while the trader seeks information on and heavily regards the short term and may utilize information generated outside the market as a backdrop. This statement introduces the second distinction between trading and investing.

Management

Both traders and investors manage their decision-making process and hence their position through or over time. But because of the type of information each focuses on, each must employ a different management approach. Managing a trade differs from managing an investment in that in managing an investment through time, one does not employ a "hands on," near-term approach, but is more passive, employing a long timeframe. (Either price rises above value, or changes take place in cost or demand, or management changes are effected, or any combination of these occurrences which increase the value of the property take place.) In other words, when investing, as defined in Graham and Dodd's *Security Analysis,* actively monitoring the market is not required. A person enters an investment because information outside the market (as opposed to market-generated information) indicates an opportunity to buy price below value; the market is then expected to "carry the day" and produce price at or above value results. The position is held through time so that the opportunity can evolve and the rest of the market participants can recognize the security's value. Meanwhile, the investor actively monitors the outside-the-market information as it is updated. So long as updates indicate that the undervalued situation is intact, the position is held. If updates of the outside-the-market information indicate that the underlying conditions are changing, the position is reevaluated, and it is either kept and reevaluated again, or exited.

In contrast, managing a trade requires a more "hands on," active management approach than managing an investment, as market-generated information is updated with the unfolding of every time-price opportunity. Just as the investor updates his assessment of the investment with new information, so does the trader. Thus, because of the frequency of information, the trader is by definition an active manager. He tends to have a shorter timeframe, especially for tolerating a negative performance, since he is made aware of a changing situation much sooner. Thus, in trading, near-term management is essential, because the opportunity is not necessarily presumed to carry the day and changes in the situation are quickly reflected in market-generated information.

To fully clarify the distinction, consider the management approach employed by the trader with the shortest timeframe — the local scalper in a futures pit. The local scalper seeks to enter the marketplace only to buy at the bid and/or sell at the offer. This "edge" he receives for making the trade provides a period of time from which he can operate in a low-risk fashion under current conditions. He does not initiate a position because of price being below value, or monumental changes due to an emerging technology or increased demand — occurrences which may take years to fully unfold. Thus, he does not presume the situation will carry the day. Nor is the local's management approach one which relies on predictions. His management approach involves his actively monitoring the market, buying at the bid and selling at the offer, seeking only risk-free capital exposure and monitoring the market forward for change.

As he detects the slightest market change, he reevaluates his position. His goal was to be able to offset the trade profitably as soon as possible within the timeframe the edge allows him, or at least to be able to exit the trade at the same price before the conditions change and force him to take a loss. In other words, he tries — for the majority of his trades — to either make a profit or break even and not take one or a series of losses. His success rests on his willingness to exit positions without waiting for the market to show him a loss.

The Concept of Free Exposure

Because of his ability combined with the frequency with which he may update his situational assessment, he is in the best situation that can face an investor/trader. He "buys" what can be termed "free exposure" in the marketplace: over a large sample size he has the chance to make money without the risk of losing it. This is because once he initiates a trade, he has the luxury of a certain period of time required to exit the trade without a loss, if he so desires. In this process, he may be using as background some outside investment information that may be available, but before making the trade and while holding the position, he primarily relies on his sense of the ongoing condition of the marketplace, garnered from market-generated information, to activate his decisions. [8]

Any successful trader approaches the marketplace from a risk standpoint similar to that of the local: he wishes only to enter those positions where he can enter the market, and either profit or extract himself from his position, if he has any adverse assessment of his situation, without facing a loss in capital. In other words, like the local, he is willing to either take a profit or get out breaking even or with a small loss, avoiding a large loss. But his approach does not include a willingness to "take a profit or loss, whichever comes first." He tries — through management — to gain free exposure. In other words, he is not trying to predict the future, but merely to understand what is going on in the present and have either a break-even or profitable situation to take advantage of.

The investor, on the other hand, also seeks a period of free exposure. He hopes that the undervalued opportunity that he detects in the marketplace — which is based on information outside of the marketplace and overlaid upon it — can carry the day. He manages the position according to the frequency of his information — not market-generated information, but information outside the marketplace (balance sheets, monthly sales reports, market forecasts, management, research and development). In suffering exposure, he exits the trade in the following situations: the strong investor gives the market a period of time in which to unfold, but exits when the outside information changes, making it doubtful that the favorable event will take place; the investor who is less sure of his value assessment will often exit using a monetary rule of a certain percentage of his capital impaired, a procedure similar to the already discredited stop-loss order.

The approach of both the investor and trader calls for knowledge. The trader needs knowledge of the market-generated information while the investor needs knowledge of information outside the market pertaining to the asset's value. Both need to understand present tense conditions which support their information source, because monitoring their position calls for noting any changes and being able to relate them to one's previous determination. Yet neither the investor nor the trader is willing to blindly take a profit or a loss — whichever comes first. This is a choice forced on individuals willing to take a chance without knowledge.

With this knowledge of the difference between approaches, a successful investor should be able to adjust and tailor his strategy to become a successful trader, and vice versa.

This distinction was provided because the majority of individuals are using an investing approach when they should be trading and vice versa. In other words, the current trading approach manages a trade as if it were an investment. It does not stress monitoring the market, but ignores market-generated information. A proper trading approach requires much more management than is generally understood, and that is why the current state of the financial industry discourages de jure trading, encouraging de facto investing in its place. It is obvious that both approaches call for informed management. Both will fail without it.

The Current State of Trading vs. Market Logic

This leads to the comparision of the current state of trading decision
making and the sound, logical decision-making approach. Like the
difference between trading and investing, the difference between the
current, illogical approach and the logical approach is the type of
information used and how it is analyzed within a decision-making
framework or process (e.g., outside information related to the market
versus market-generated information related to it).

In the current state, almost all transactional information, information derived from newspapers, retrieval services, and even live quotes
disseminated by vendors, falls into the classification of information
outside the market. (Most people are surprised that live quotes are not
included in the other category, market-generated information. But
upon examination, live market quotes are not formulated into a
statistically measurable and logically sound arrangement of data which
provides information.) In other words, transactional information is
either presented in tabular, numerical form or else reorganized and
presented in graphic chart form.

Regardless, the market is conventionally presented as a price against
a price. Past price high, low and close points are then related to the
current situation and used to predict the probable course of future
prices. What is needed is to capture and define the situation as it is at
present, and present a price against its logical context (a price distinction). The only database that currently offers comprehensive market
information formulated in this way is the Chicago Board of Trade's
Liquidity Data Bank and Market Profile.

Consequently, there is a dearth of information which the trader in
the current state uses to manage his trading. But little is available which
provides a framework from which he can monitor live market data with
the goal of market understanding and hence risk-free trading for capital
preservation. The current approach to trading is one where the majority
cannot differentiate price from value, and will consequently have many
problems. With the current approach, normal individuals essentially
lose before they even start. With this current approach, only the very
exceptional have a chance to succeed.

The Perils of Predicting

Many of the problems caused by the current state of trading/investing
are an outgrowth of attempting to predict the future in a market of
uncertainty. Because traders and investors characteristically attempt to
predict, many practices have developed which are supported by logical
myths and are clearly counterproductive for anyone wishing to improve
his results.

One such myth involves the use of stops as a defensive strategy aimed at capital preservation, which has already been discussed. When predicting, it is usual to have a point at which a loss of capital will be accepted, and to place stop-loss orders at this point. The placement of stops for capital preservation has been accepted as a management tool when in fact it does not come from market-generated information, but rather is an artificial parameter. Using stops is management by price and worst-case dollar losses rather than management by monitoring price over time. Furthermore, there can be no logical reason for such a decision-making parameter. No timeframe can be established (only a price frame), and adjustments are not easily made, since no thought is given to change. This approach creates no desire to obtain market-generated information. It is an approach adopted by those who often seek unrealistic dollar goals rather than free exposure. The use of stops abdicates the ability to differentiate between opportunities.

A myth which has fostered the use of stops is that those who predict and employ stops can lose much more often than five times out of ten and still have positive results, so long as the losses are small and the winning positions are held and ridden. Yet to perform worse than five out of ten is to willingly accept less than happenstance. Winning less often than losing but letting profits run is fine in theory, but very tough in actual practice. Losing repeatedly puts the normal individual under unrelenting stress. Thus, such an approach requires individual strength to an extent not usually realized.

Successful predicting can often be of little value. Many market participants use information outside the marketplace overlaid on the market — where this assessment is correct in a broad sense — and still fail to capitalize on that knowledge. For example, it was no secret that the market was in a broad advance in raw materials during the 1970s. The difficult task was successfully implementing an approach, when the volatility of daily activity was such that the correct position could not easily be held through time. This illustrates the problem associated with predicting even when it is correct, versus having market under-standing and managing with market-generated information.

Predicting in a market of uncertainty puts most individuals in a situation where they do not benefit from the learning experience, since they are not actively monitoring the market. They do not consider the storehouse of experience they have built up as consumers in other markets and do not apply it to their operation in the organized markets.

An analogy contrasting the current state of trading the market to the desired and successful approach involves the modus operandi of a physician treating a critically ill patient. The doctor does not try to predict what the patient's situation will be in days or weeks, much to the consternation of the patient's family. Rather, the doctor monitors change over time, specifically, changes in the patient's vital signs and symptoms over time. He looks for signs of weakness and strength, weakness accepted versus weakness rejected. He monitors median measurements for the patient's vital signs, looking for a trend of increasing strength or increasing weakness to report to the family.

To continue the analogy a bit, consider the folly if a doctor were to use the approach inherent in a stop order — accepting the patient's getting better or worse, but only whichever comes first. While treating the patient, if vital signs dropped to a certain point or if symptoms grew worse to the point of the stop, the doctor would order the patient a coffin and give up. In reality, doctors know that all situations differ and the patient's setback might only be temporary. When a setback occurs, a doctor searches for its cause while considering what might counter it.

The individual who has a market understanding need not resort to predicting the future, but can monitor the market in much the same way the doctor monitors his patient.

Some Thoughts on Technical Analysis

Technical analysis and other forecasting indicators as a "for profit" industry have been quite successful and readily accepted. One might say that technical analysis products such as high-low-close charts, similar graphic quotation machines, etc., have been in a twenty-year secular bull market which began in the mid-1960s. This is because technical analysis and other such indicators as products are what the "market" wants.

However, such tools do not give most participants what they need. Technical analysis and other tools focus on price as a single, clear indicator. But when acting based on price information alone, the individual tends to be late rather than early, and often is simply incorrect. Technical analysis casts traders in a mode where, by concentrating on price, they are abandoning time and its controlling and defining influence. This causes them to mistakenly treat all situations similarly, when in fact, their own experience indicates otherwise. In other words, identical price parameters often will trigger trades which yield different results.

It has been demonstrated that organized markets are like other markets, and operate as they have been operating in the normal course of business for centuries. It might be valuable, then, to consider how business decisions are generated.

In normal businesses, the successful owner and/or manager himself routinely makes key buying, selling, expanding, contracting and financing decisions based on information. This decision-making process does not rely on a single indicator; nor does it rely on a set of similar indicators which have demonstrated unreliability in the past. It does not rely on making a prediction and then acting, with a passive management approach, either. Instead, the successful owner and/or manager takes what might be termed a checklist or spreadsheet approach, identifying the variables which logically impact the problem or potential gain at hand, weighting their respective importance to the decision at hand, and monitoring their up-to-the-moment status against their recent past. He will therefore be analyzing numerous small, subtle indicators.

For example, if he were to consider expanding his sales operation, before making the decisions he would probably consider such things as company morale, recent sales growth, profit margins, quality control, anticipated cost increases if expansion takes place, anticipated increases in shipping costs, the percentage increase in capacity his current operation can handle, etc. It is useful when reading the history of the great mercantile empires of the past, to ponder what considerations were investigated prior to a business decision.

If the spreadsheet approach is what owners and managers use in other businesses, why has it not been applied to market analysis on a widespread basis before this? The answer is obvious. Technical analysis provides what traders and investors want rather than what they need. We would all like simple, straightforward indicators rather than have to assess numerous complex issues, looking at each within the context of the situation at hand and thus having to weight each in importance accordingly. Technical analysis offers what we all would find ideal -- if it worked consistently -- in making any business decision.

What a trader really needs is what every businessman needs: a decision support system which, because it is based on his own observation of reality, allows him to know he is identifying all or most of the elements which will either impact the future or indicate the present situation as it relates to the problem or potential. The businessman then traces back (monitors) how and under what circumstances each of these elements has performed up through the present, thus providing a framework for analyzing information and drawing logical conclusions. Technical analysis and other forecasting tools have a tremendous potential when they can be formulated to service this need.

Making decisions based on technical analysis is highly subjective and can be used successfully by some, as can anything. However, consider the following questions when pondering the added value provided to the trading/investing decision-making process by technical analysis or any other approach to markets:

1. Is it an organized, logical arrangement and presentation of data for a logical purpose?

2. Does this arrangement employ accepted statistical tools which facilitate inspection, measurement, interpretation and valid conclusions?

3. In providing information, does this arrangement represent conclusions that can be statistically supported?

4. Does this arrangement define, organize and capture all change in the market?

5. In representing market activity, does it provide all the valuable information obtainable?

6. Does this arrangement facilitate interpretation, understanding and decision support rather than merely make predictions?

7. Is this presentation of data representative of market (or general business) logic?

8. Does it treat all prices equally?

9. Does it misrepresent prices as market activity?

10. Does it differentiate between opportunities?

11. Does it define market-created opportunities?

12. Does it differentiate between the conditions, allowing detection of major market changes over time? (For instance, the conditions in the 1970s were not the same as those in the 1980s.)

13. Does it funnel masses of data to a point or single entity, when in fact these data should be examined for subtle changes over a large sample size?

14. Does it portray a large, clear and single decision-making indicator (price), when in fact, in a competitive situation, all decision-making indicators are small and subtle?

15. Is it only applicable for large samples, or can a reliable reading be conducted on a small sample size?

16. Is it hampered by happenstance?

17. Are the indicators late? Does this cause a person who is

naturally (humanly) prone to be late to accentuate this problem?

18. Does it force people to use stops, setting artificial parameters?

19. Does it encourage thinking for oneself or developing experience?

20. Does it present buying rallies and selling breaks as "going with the market" when in fact a rally is advertising for sellers?

21. Does it allow people to monitor or manage with time, as markets do?

22. Does it put the majority of participants in a situation where they have a statistical advantage over the large sample size?

23. Does it put the majority of participants in a situation where they can win before they start?

24. As currently practiced, has technical analysis changed the results of those who have been exposed to it?

25. Is technical analysis conceptually logical?

Technical analysis needs to be able to incorporate market-generated information on small as well as large sample sizes that will allow people to monitor and adjust their decisions on a sound and logical basis. With these questions as an indication of areas for improvement, technical analysis and all other forms of market analysis can over time evolve into a more logical, consistent, practical and hence valuable tool for those in the marketplace.

The Logical Approach

The logical approach understands that the current state is illogical, that people for the most part do not understand what it is they are doing (and how it is in actuality being done) nor the implications of the tools they are working with. The logical approach understands, explains and allows for everything. It requires a market understanding as has been discussed, a sound trading strategy and an acknowledgment of the human factor.

The logical approach rests on the following oft-repeated facts:

To be consistent, market participants need a thought process which establishes one or more logical reasons for arriving at any decision, particularly a buy or sell decision. The vast majority of participants do not provide for themselves the framework to do this because they assume disorganization or randomness of price as a given in every organized marketplace, rather than structuring or organizing market-generated data. While they unconsciously are able to ascertain value with a high time-price occurrence in simple and everyday markets, they rarely apply this and other logical insights to the seemingly chaotic organized financial markets. Indeed, when individuals apply the same principles they unknowingly use in other, less complicated markets to the organized marketplaces such as the futures and stock markets, they find that these principles hold true. They realize that despite superficial differences, all markets are alike and their practical, logical insights hold true for even the most complex of markets. Further, the majority of participants do not realize the interconnection of all things; principles that hold true in nature and in areas of human endeavor, particularly business, hold true in markets, particularly the organized markets. The market may be outwardly chaotic, but, as a balancing mechanism, it has an inward sense of order which allows individuals to statistically examine it using the bell curve.

Price and value differ in all markets. Through work, value can always be ascertained, either from information outside the market -- in the case of securities -- or from market-generated information. Further, price is a variable, while time is a constant and in order to build a trading strategy around a market understanding, a participant needs to use a unit of time as a constant with which to measure price activity. As already mentioned, market logic dictates that a solid trading strategy in any market begins with an understanding of the market, which again rests on the equation,

Price + time = volume = market acceptance = value.

In other words, since the market regulates itself through time, to be in step with the market, the individual must also monitor himself in terms of time. In doing so, the trader will be providing himself with enough time to assess the market unemotionally, to understand where trade is taking place and hence where a value area is being established, and then to act accordingly. The equation for results introduced the third section of this book:

Your market understanding x (you + your trading strategy) = results.

We have discussed the two basic types of approaches any participant can employ and we have discussed what each requires in terms of this equation.

This equation goes much further; it defines exactly why most market participants defeat themselves in the exchange marketplace: First of all, they have a poor understanding of the purpose of the marketplace, and the needs and goals which motivate market participants. Nor can they locate and place prices as distinguished from value as expressed in the transactional data known as market activity. They cannot separate the activity of the short timeframe participant from that of the long timeframe participant, and therefore cannot make sound, low-risk decisions on a regular basis.

Secondly, most participants have a poor trading/investing strategy which does not take into account an understanding of themselves as human beings combined with an understanding of the tool they are using, and thus, their strategy regularly asks too much of themselves.

Lastly, they do not understand or monitor themselves for personal patterns, nor do they discipline themselves, so they do not put themselves in positions where they regularly make rational, nonemotional decisions based on their market understanding. They also fail to recognize the importance of their experience in other everyday markets, and the value this experience (or any experience) holds in the organized markets.

Taking action based on an equation for results puts reality above all else, and enables the percentages to be put in favor of the individual, allowing the average decision maker to win on the grind. It does this by allowing him to break down each of the equation's three components for close examination and potential improvement. The next logical step for the individual seeking to improve results is one of the most difficult tasks in the trading process, namely, learning how to think in an objective and critical sense, and doing so when examining each part of the equation as it applies to himself. That is, now that he has a framework from which to analyze the variables of his trading or investing success or failure, he must examine the market and his understanding of it, the potential and necessary trading strategies, and especially himself in an empirical, pragmatic and creative manner in order to develop a consistent thought and action process in trading.

These issues must be examined and considered extensively by each individual himself. As in many areas of life, there are no right answers, and no one other than each individual can determine what is right for him. All successful market participants have learned how to think, act and rely on themselves, first to come up with answers to the various components which combine to spell success or failure, and then to implement trading decisions in the markets. In other words, each participant seeking success must develop the ability to monitor the market and himself by continually observing, recording, reflecting, analyzing and evaluating his beliefs and approach. By doing so, an individual gains experience and insights into change in the market and himself, and can thus become self-reliant. But this is not enough. He must observe, reflect and think. Observations, reflections and thoughts must then be placed in a structure. And he must continually be rethinking and reevaluating, recognizing mistakes and altering his course, and refining his trading thought process.

---

[5] Structure is defined by price over time, creating transactional volume.

[6] In the absence of definitions, misconceptions grow. For example, the conventional wisdom states that investing is low risk, while trading is the opposite -- replete with risk. Indeed, "investing" is portrayed as a respectable endeavor fit for gentlemen and scholar alike, while "trading" is portrayed in opposite terms, carrying with it a stigma of opportunism and considered the domain of the boor.

[7] Certainly, the conventional differentiation between investors and traders can be made: investors wish to own the item whereas traders buy to sell. However, the agreement can be made that both buy to own, with an intent to sell for a profit. These distinctions thus become one of timeframes, i.e., how long the holding period will be.

[8] A successful trader, like the investor, will hold his position over time when his information indicates that the position is working well and the opportunity will carry the day. The trader particularly (rather than only, as is the case with the investor) succeeds when an overwhelming trending opportunity occurs. But the trader is usually far more active than the investor, because trending markets which reward patience are but a small percentage of all opportunities -- most opportunities call for a combination of many active skills, rather than only for patience.

12

A MARKET UNDERSTANDING

Developing a market understanding is a large undertaking which can be begun by reviewing the first two sections of this book.

13

YOU

With a good background in market understanding, it is possible to have an up-to-the-minute, 100% understanding of a particular market at any given time. And every participant with a good market understanding should employ a sound trading strategy (detailed in the next chapter) which over time should mean success. But, as stated in the beginning of this section, successful trading requires an understanding of much more than the market and a sound trading strategy. It requires making sound decisions on a regular basis. Yet most traders concentrate primarily on discovering the direction they feel the market is headed, giving diminished attention to their trading strategy, and the least amount of attention to themselves and how they function as humans and confident, rational decision makers.

Yet it is the last category — the "you" part of the equation — which is the most important element in the trading process. Everything else can be learned. Most participants in every marketplace fail because even when they have an understanding of the market, they do not understand or monitor themselves, and they cannot discipline and control themselves. Therefore, they cannot put themselves in positions where they will regularly and consistently make rational, nonemotional decisions based on their market understanding. In other words, the weakest link in a trader's approach to a market is often himself. Overcoming this truism is by far the most difficult challenge every trader faces.

The first step a trader must make when considering how to adjust for and improve the "you quotient" is to realize that he is a member of the human race. In other words, he must compare and contrast himself to the frailties and strengths of human beings as a class. While he cannot put himself outside the human race, he may deviate from the norm in certain areas.

Some broad observations of the characteristics of the human race at this point in our evolution include:

Man's powers of observation are no longer critical to his survival and thus have declined through underuse.

Man's ability to think for himself analytically has also declined through lack of use. The structure of civilized society combined with technology's impact on humankind's environment does not encourage either observation or independent thinking.

Man as a class would prefer to be led and told what to do rather than think for himself. The success of modern advertising attests to this.

Man as a class is inconsistent in his behavior: he will respond differently to the same situation and set of data depending on mood, stimuli, etc. Furthermore, his capacity and perceptions will change throughout different stages in his life.

Man as a class does not enjoy the feeling of being either physically or ideologically alone, especially in stressful conditions.

Man as a class does not want to be left out or left behind.

Man as a whole tends not to have an accurate sense of his own self-worth. He tends to overinflate or underinflate his self-worth, thus impacting his perceptions of reality.

Man as a class has a natural tendency towards lack of self-confidence.

Man as a class is jealous of those who have more than he.

Man as a class often thinks he is improving when he is not.

These characteristics combine to complicate man's decision-making ability. His perspective is regularly clouded by hesitation, euphoric impulsiveness and overconfidence, anxiety, ambition, prejudice, melancholy, self-gratification, laziness, jealousy and egotism. Minimizing these tendencies of modern human nature is the most difficult task for anyone to overcome.

But despite these problems, modern man as a class also has numerous assets. He can often successfully think — when forced to — and he can manage himself and often lead others when circumstances are right. He can learn from his mistakes and experiences, as well as the mistakes and experiences of others. And he has an amazing resilience, which, combined with the ability to learn, teach and lead, allows him and his society to adapt and change when the environment calls for it. Thus, civilized society is not a closed society, it is flexible and open to change and improvement.

Knowing Yourself and Your Patterns

It is important to study your character, personality, and judgment under varying conditions, just as you would study market activity. Self-study is important not only for personal development, but for development of your trading, since how far you can succeed in the latter is directly proportional to the extent of your development in the former.

The challenge which every market participant and every introspective person faces, then, involves acknowledging himself as a thinking, feeling human being. To do this you must know your abilities. This self-knowledge enables you to be able to stay within your abilities, and comes only from monitoring yourself for patterns, just as you would monitor other market participants or market activity. In other words, every market participant needs to study himself and his trading patterns, with the goal of understanding himself, his patterns, and his capabilities, and with the ultimate goal of using this information to improve his trading and/or investing performance.

One valuable ability which aids this study might be termed behavioral perception, the ability to study the behavior of price, time, other participants and yourself. To cultivate this ability, you need to be alert enough to make observations, and have the desire to remember them, the energy to reflect on them, and the intelligence necessary to place them in their proper structure and evaluate them correctly. This process produces both a market understanding and self-knowledge which reduces risk. When combined with the discipline provided by a well-developed "you," it totally eliminates risk over a large sample size of trades.

How do you study your own characteristics to discover how and where you differ from the crowd? Simply consider what you do not do well. Each of us has many things he does not do well. And what can you do well? What are your behavioral patterns? How do you perform when you are tired? Are you more objective after a vacation? After taking profits versus after taking losses? Can you easily reverse your position in the market, or do you feel uncomfortable doing so? Only you can ascertain your abilities by looking at yourself, and you should probably reach your conclusions based only on your own observations.

The next step in understanding yourself and your behavioral patterns lies in seeing and facing reality. In other words, after you have critically found and defined your capabilities and personal patterns, be satisfied with what you find. Concentrate on being happy with yourself. While trying to improve your ability to handle situations that you can not currently handle well, strive to understand and gravitate toward those market opportunities which you know you can handle well.

Acknowledge that you will make mistakes, and that making the wrong decision is much easier than making the correct one, although you won't always know simply by the outcome. For example, the tired trader often finds he does not really control himself very well, thereby making emotionally motivated decisions, which, no matter if they result in profit or loss, are nevertheless mistakes. (In other words, do not trade when in a weakened state or when particular skills or capabilities which you find yourself lacking are called for. Don't expect too much from yourself, the market or others.)

The goal of this entire exercise? Simply put, when you have an understanding of the market and an understanding of your own capabilities, you can begin to match your capabilities to the opportunities the market regularly presents that are suited to what you can handle. This brings in the point that there are two things you need to consider before initiating a trade: the market opportunity (preferably rating it and then weighting it; see the next chapter) and how well you are trading at the time that opportunity comes up. Sometimes, when the opportunity is special, you will want to stretch your range and attempt to operate above what your past has indicated. But this should be the exception rather than the rule. True self-knowledge and strength is demonstrated when you can feel good about passing up some very attractive opportunities which your current mental, emotional or physical state or capabilities makes you feel uncomfortable in tackling.

Avoiding Emotional Decisions

It is important to remember that in all areas of practical life, reason and logic are regularly overwhelmed by the natural tendencies of hesitation, euphoric overconfidence, anxiety, ambition, prejudice, melancholy, laziness, jealousy, egotism, and the need for self-gratification. These tendencies occur in individuals involved in the marketplace as they do elsewhere. Indeed, they may be compounded in the futures markets and the investment field in general, since when the individual uses leverage, success can spell quick wealth while failure can mean correspondingly quick financial ruin. Such possibilities create anxiety, particularly in the decision maker who is less informed. Clearly, one of the most difficult challenges the trader regularly faces is to avoid making decisions not firmly grounded in reason or logic.

The first step toward avoiding emotional decisions is having a market understanding which provides sufficient information to allow the trader to confidently generate his own decisions. Having a market understanding allows the trader to develop an approach to the market and a trading style that is dependent on himself, not others.

Another way to decrease the propensity for emotionalism is to slow down. In order to achieve consistently successful results, you certainly need to originate your own ideas, but then also have time in which to carry those ideas into action. Trading in the instant does not provide time to make a relaxed decision without undue pressure, since you are always reacting to what somebody else has done, and therefore are subject to substantial stress. One way to avoid making emotional trading decisions is to trade from a longer timeframe, never reacting to a single price or a single bit of market-generated information.

A third way to decrease emotionalism is to realize that you cannot be better than you normally are over time and that your trading strategy has to reflect this. In other words, the percentage of time in which you can be at your best is limited, and by acknowledging this you can lower your expectations of your performance. Most participants ask themselves to be at their peak potential all the time, inadvertently placing themselves under great pressure.

Another point to be made is that the current success level that the individual controls is not entirely in his hands. The attractiveness of market-created opportunities varies. Thus, superior results cannot be attributed to your abilities alone, but rather to the matching of your talents to the particular opportunities available.

The last point to be made is that few humans can trade unemotionally when concentrating solely on money or the financial aspect of their market operations. Concentrate instead on monitoring market-generated information, your behavior patterns, and other factors involved in making a trading or investing decision.

The Trader's Biggest Problem

Conventional wisdom emphasizes that the emotions of fear and greed motivate every market and that these two emotions are the trader's greatest enemy. These statements do not display a deep understanding of human psychology. The key emotional factor in market behavior is also the biggest roadblock to effective decision making. It is the hardest emotion for every trader to control: the propensity toward hesitation, toward being late. The average market participant is always late — whether in initiating a position or exiting a profitable or losing position. Rather than greed, the opposing emotion tends to be impulsiveness, a "rushing in blindly" that is usually accompanied by a euphoria or emotional high that often follows success in the marketplace. Both responses cause reason and disciplined, logical decision making to lapse, often causing the participant to become vulnerable to taking action as an emotional response.

Traders and investors, as humans, want company, and it is a rare person who does not have any problem being alone in a major decision. Yet opportunities at their early stage, by definition, are not going to have a lot of people taking advantage of them and in fact are going to have many people doing the opposite. Thus, not hesitating when acting logically is difficult due to basic human nature. It asks for an uncharacteristic human response. It is for this reason that making the right decision and acting on it when called to is often very difficult. Hesitating and consequently being late are more comfortable and reassuring than being early. This is often because of self-doubt or fear of going against the crowd. In other words, hesitation is not a problem when the trade is obvious (and over), because the decision is not one which goes against the crowd.

Euphoric impulsiveness is caused when you are exuberant and overconfident from a recent success. Euphoric impulsiveness causes you to get careless and overconfident and begin to see things that aren't there.

It is imperative to be aware of your individual propensity for having such emotional lapses. Hesitation usually occurs when an individual is not performing well, while the opposite is true for euphoric impulsiveness.

When one is doing well one tends not to hesitate. One way to control your propensity toward hesitation and being late is to blank out all past negative experiences and all past incorrect decisions. Seek to be positive about everything and have no fear. Big doubts will not help generate effective, rational decisions. Instead of negative experiences, concentrate on the present situation and on visualizing an unfolding market.

Once you are aware of your individual propensities, strive to react to an opportunity logically but automatically, like the tennis player who gets an opportunity to crash the net and put away the point, but only if he reacts automatically in taking advantage of the opportunity. In other words, reacting as such must almost become a reflex. Hesitation in either sports or trading may mean that the opportunity is over before one has had a chance to capitalize on it. On the other hand, being impulsive, or acting without reason or patience, is also clearly a major fault. The key is to visualize several possible scenarios, to have solid reasons to act, and to be early, yet patient. Monitor yourself to be consistent at this.

It is important to remember that regardless of your propensity, it will provide both a zone of benefit and a zone of harm over the gamut of decisions. For example, the person who hesitates wants to be sure that he is correct, much like anyone reading this book or attending a class on trading technique. He is not by nature impulsive, and therefore benefits in such situations which do not require instant decisions. A conflict occurs when the same individual is forced to operate in a very short timeframe situation where hesitancy can spell disaster. In other words, hesitation has its benefits for the second or longer timeframe participant while impulsiveness benefits the shorter or day timeframe participant.

While you may either be hesitant or impulsive, one characteristic will be more dominant and should be used to the fullest in situations where benefits accrue. Likewise, the dominant tendency should be neutralized where such a reaction may harm. The issue is not to change, or develop the ability to shift your natural tendency. Doing so would put you in a position of working with a variable rather than a known constant. In other words, you cannot ask yourself to flip back and forth between situations which require hesitation and those which require impulsiveness, and handle each situation as adeptly and aggressively. You do not have to be outside your normal pattern of behavior to maximize your potential effectiveness as a trading/investing decision maker.

As you can see and probably already know all too well, effective decision making is very difficult. Again, it is so because it runs counter to man's natural emotional tendencies. After you have a market understanding and are confident in your analysis, the remaining stumbling block is major but subtle: you must teach yourself to do what you know you should do. A point of comfort should be taken knowing that often, the more difficult a decision is to reach, the more correct it is. Regardless of the difficulty, though, personal control in the decision-making process is paramount. Once an individual has a good market understanding, he may spend 15% of his energy analyzing the market and 85% working on disciplining himself. Usually, the successful trader and investor, the person who regularly makes the difficult and correct decisions, is fighting to control himself, yet never outwardly displaying the battle.

Change

Knowing yourself and your tendencies is important since it allows you to accept your characteristics as constants, thereby allowing you to accept opportunities that require or feature those traits. However, it is important to recognize that you and your capabilities will vary from day to day, week to week, and year to year.

As stated in the introduction to this section, human beings are constantly in flux. In other words, they are not naturally consistent; they change due to different stimuli and different moods, throughout the various stages of life. Several assertions are about to be made which are not based on stereotyping, but rather on observations of the majority. Clearly, they will not hold true for everyone but will illuminate transition for many.

Characteristically, the beginning part of life is ruled by the subconscious, so younger or less experienced traders tend not to have a controlling fear of the consequences of their actions, and tend toward euphoric impulsiveness. The middle part of life, on the other hand, tends to focus on avoidance of painful or negative experiences, such as the aggravation that a monetary loss causes, and one's conscious negative experiences tends to rule over the subconscious. In other words, hesitation as a pattern of behavior sets in very easily. Consequently, younger traders tend not to exercise enough caution while middle-aged traders often tend to be too cautious. In the last part of life for most people, the subconscious and conscious become integrated and are working together. Major financial responsibilities and commitments have been fulfilled and financial gain takes on a less emotional meaning and becomes more of a game.

The point is that you should recognize that your capabilities will vary from day to day and year to year. You should strive to build on experience with the market and yourself and learn, but keep in mind that you need to be flexible and alert to the abnormal, since both the market and you are changing over time. The informed participant is constantly aware of where he is in his life, guarding against his impulsiveness and lack of fear on the one hand, and his overly restrained conscious self and the resulting self-doubt on the other.

Getting to Where You Belong

Many of the points mentioned are superfluous to certain very fortunate people. But these people are few in number. By far the majority fail to analyze themselves critically and map out their own course in life, a course chosen not to imitate others, but to maximize their individual strengths and minimize their weaknesses. Short-circuited by society's expectations and chosen routes, they don't end up where they are comfortable and can function happily at their highest level to provide the most value to society. But those who have arrived enjoy vast insights into themselves, their needs and the true meaning of success.

Getting to where you belong in life is very difficult. Consequently, the person who has found himself, mapped out his own course and then has arrived, is doing what he wants to do. He is low-keyed and even-keeled. He has a lot of self-confidence and has no need to try to impress others. It is because he is very self-assured and confident of his abilities that he doesn't have to prove anything to others. Interestingly, the background of many of today's very successful traders and investors as a group demonstrates the ability to migrate to where they belong — where they are happiest — in life.

The highest level of realization and self-sufficiency is attained by defining and then attempting to fulfill your own concept of success. But before defining it, you must understand that gaining it requires both a great amount of self-knowledge and the rare ability to act on this knowledge.

Stress

One conventional wisdom has it that trading in any market, especially futures, is an especially stressful business. Stress is caused by living with problems. Rather than live with a problem, you should seek to eliminate it. In other words, the only stress you should expect from being an active market participant occurs when you are wrong but do not get out of the position. The human element in you will register stress when your subconscious is being overruled by your conscious level. This comes from experience or a great deal of exposure in the marketplace. As you understand yourself, you will naturally discover how you feel when you have a bad position on and do nothing about it. Seek to train yourself to know that you are wrong by being in tune with your body's reactions — especially your reactions to stress.

Conclusion

This chapter has focused on the conclusively variable element in trading, that element we define as "you." The next section discusses strategic considerations you should ponder prior to and while you are taking action in the market. These two sections overlap to a significant extent, which is a reflection of the interrelationship between an understanding of yourself, and the strategic implications which come out of this understanding.

14

TRADING (AND INVESTING) STRATEGY AND TECHNIQUES

I t was pointed out earlier that very few participants can be as good as is called for in the currently accepted approaches to trading and investing. Certainly, there are those who are very successful participants who have overcome and can overcome a lack of understanding of the markets. However, these individuals are very rare, because they can function at a very high level without sufficient information and therefore under tremendous pressure. Few of us actually understand (before discovering the hard way), how difficult it is to be such a participant on a consistent basis.

How then, is the average person to succeed as a market participant? In a word, strategy.

Strategy, in a general sense, is the modus operandi an individual chooses, believing that employing it will help him steer clear of the barriers between him and his goal. A trading strategy is nothing more than a game plan of universal principles and tactics which is mapped out before trading is considered.

Strategy involves developing an approach to the market which will neutralize an individual's human frailties, those tendencies which prevent him from attaining successful results. Your trading strategy, as a subset of your overall market approach, must therefore take into account your individual personal, physical and psychological strengths and weaknesses. Thus, your trading strategy must be tailored only for you. It must be developed from the perspective of what you yourself currently are, not what you would like to be or what any other person is.

By adjusting for your market understanding and your "you," a sound strategy allows you to win over the large sample size of trades. Once it is mapped out, adherence to the strategy should be strictly self-enforced. It should be enforced just as strenuously decades into your successful trading-investing career as it is in the early days immediately following its development.

This done, assuming he has the self-discipline necessary to follow the plan, the individual puts himself in the position of "winning before he begins." In other words, you understand what you're working with, and are prepared so that over the large sample size or longer period of time, you will necessarily achieve the goal. Hence, a subtle benefit of mapping out a strategy is that it allows you not to be overly concerned with failures in the small sample size.

Structuring Success

When structuring a strategy, the challenge every market participant faces is starting out. Starting out is more complex than most of us first realize; if approached incorrectly, an individual's start can also easily be his finish. The "you" section of this book discusses the importance of making a critical self-assessment. Once this is done, and assuming a market understanding has been developed through observation, one should begin trading or investing.

One of the central theses in this book has been the universality of markets and of practical existence in general. Illustrating another universality, starting out in trading/investing is like starting out in any other business. You, as a beginning market participant, should consider your market operations as a new business. You can be considered as the new factory. Intelligent management always strives first to get the product out of the factory easily and efficiently before trying to boost production. Once you are able to take the raw materials (the market, your understanding of it, and yourself) and produce the product (consistent profits over a reasonable sample size) then and only then can you boost volume. In other words, it is wise to trade in the smallest possible unit size until the learning curve has risen and flattened out and profits are made regularly.

Furthermore, as a mature market participant you should continue to monitor yourself like corporate management should monitor the factory: you have a potential, a capacity and an operating level. The key is to match yourself up with opportunity, taking into account your abilities at the moment. In other words, you should trade at or below capacity most of the time, just as the factory should be run at or below capacity most of the time. If you are trading below capacity at your operating level, there is less stress, and you will most likely make a higher percentage of nonemotional decisions on a consistent basis than otherwise.

The point is, the successful trader must become his own manager and strive to improve in all three levels. You must strive to build a bigger, more efficient trading ability boosting potential and capacity. You may then safely boost your operating level. As an intelligently managed factory, you should reserve your potential for the opportunities of windfall profit nature, since no plant can operate at its potential for long without serious problems.

Logical Market Realizations

A solid trading strategy necessitates several realizations. The first and probably the most important as far as trading strategy is involved is this: A participant with a solid trading strategy must always have a sound reason for making every buy-sell decision, a reason based on his market understanding.

A second realization is that opportunities differ and hence the approach, choice of tools and size must reflect the particular opportunity. In other words, the opportunity dictates the trading strategy. Thus, the tool for situation (futures contract, option, outright cash transaction, etc.) and the size of the transaction (small, medium, or maximum) must depend on a self-generated evaluation of the situation.

A third realization which has been mentioned under the "you" section is that the enlightened trader not only understands the attractiveness of the opportunity; he understands and applies the proper strategy not only to the opportunity as it relates to the market but, most importantly, to himself. Your evaluation must take into account an assessment of the market plus the degree of market understanding possessed at a particular moment, your recent performance, recent and current comfort level, and total financial condition. A solid trading strategy is therefore individually tailored to each participant's abilities, risk tolerance, and comfort level continually as it unfolds.

Another important realization is the importance of understanding -- in a strategic sense -- the tool being used. In other words, a sound strategy allows you to be wrong on any one trade or a small series of trades without the risk of ruin. Thus, a solid trading strategy is never so aggressive that the participant becomes uncomfortable with his position, monitoring it in emotional terms, calculating the money involved, or exhibiting any other pattern which distracts from the calculated and objective decision-making process. You should be sure to evaluate and learn from your overall performance, especially the mistakes. This, over time, will provide trading experience, a development of the soundness and consistency of one's evaluation.

In order to use any tool, you must thoroughly understand the principal behind it. In a market of uncertainty, anything will work 50% of the time. Most of the tools utilized today have a degree of merit, but the failure of the knowledge of the principles involved causes that participant tool to be used out of context.

In order for a tool to have value to the user, it needs to show a consistent behavior beyond the 50-50 happenstance. For example, there are indicators which will produce results ranging forward whereby they will work 60 times out of 100 to 90 times out of 100. A common misuse of the tools will be not to go beyond and understand the situations that are most favorable for their employment. (In the final minutes of a closely contested basketball game where fouling and the ability to convert at the free throw line will be the deciding factor, which information is more valuable to the coach, knowing the free throw percentages of each individual on the opposing team for the year or knowing each individual's free throw percentages in the closing minutes of closely contested games?) It is *easier* as a human being just to accept and use for any situation a tool that works some of the time, and employ it in an indiscriminate manner all the time. Yet from a strategic sense, one should always be looking for the underlying conditions, with the goal of improving percentages.

Another major strategic realization is that all tools are going to be effective during some phases of a market, but since the conditions and behavior of every market change, so will the usefulness of every tool. Thus, it is important not only to understand your tool, and under what conditions it has a high probability of working, but also understanding the correct phase of the market it works in.

Yet another important realization: one should always be aware that the short run can be an aberration of a small sample size and that happenstance rules any market of uncertainty. In other words, success over the near term does not necessarily mean that one's strategy is correct. It is very easy to produce sought-after results while being wrong. When you are doing something that you know to be incorrect, but your mistake nevertheless yields sought-after results, do not think that the approach might be right. Avoid it in the future. In other words, any tool which you think is good may not be of any value over a large sample size.

Preventive Trading

A sound trading strategy is one in which the participant avoids trades which can result in major losses in capital. With such an approach, a trader does not need to predict the market and/or enter the market with a predetermined profit and loss objective, but to merely look for those situations that offer "free exposure." Trading for free exposure is seeking to enter into and hold a position in the market for a fixed period of time without fear of losing capital during that period. The goal of seeking risk-free exposure is not to make money on any one trade, but merely to enter a situation during which one cannot lose. Doing this automatically exercises "preventive trading."

In other words, in monitoring the condition of the market, look for signs of strength or weakness, and enter the market only when you eliminate in your mind the possibility of the market moving in one direction. An over-simplified example might be the following: the market indicates weakness and is in a long-term down auction, mainly due to initiating activity on the part of other timeframe sellers. You are looking for an opportunity to sell above value. Suppose that today the market displayed initiating selling at the top of the range, responsive buying at the bottom, and net responsive buying in the value area as indicated by a time-price opportunity (TPO) count. Next, a new item is announced which motivates a reaction on the part of the short timeframe, day timeframe participant. The market rallies a distance normal for this market for an hour's time period according to recent observations.

At this point, a short position can be entered. The market should not continue to rally, since it has rallied far enough to neutralize the news event, and the market's structure is weak to begin with. One of two things will now happen: either other timeframe sellers will enter the market, responding to price above value, or they will not. If they do, they will do so shortly, and the position will begin showing profits quickly. If they do not, loss of capital is not a major factor for the next half hour, since the market has already rallied and will most likely consolidate for a while.

Entering trades with "combinations" is a key strategy in preventive trading. In other words, in order to lessen the risk of losing capital it is important to have fall-back positions.

For example, say that the market conditions are such that in a strong down auction, there has been initiating selling at the top of the range, responsive buying at the bottom, and net responsive buying in the value area as indicated by a time-price opportunity (TPO) count. If, because of a news event, the market opens 20 tics higher the next day, one has a situation where responsive selling should be apparent. If it is not apparent early in the trading session, it can be expected at the top of the range. If it does not occur, the next fall-back position is that initiating buying is not expected at the higher prices.

Preventive trading and using combinations as trading strategies are important because they allow the individual to avoid suffering bad exposure in the marketplace. Bad exposure is bound to affect performance adversely. An example of this in sports might be the baseball players who find themselves in a position of having two strikes and no balls. They will not bat as well as they would with no strikes and three balls. If an individual constantly gets into a situation in which failure threatens, he is simply not going to do as well as he is capable of doing without the pressure.

Study Your Results

Once you are in tune with your capabilities and personal patterns, it is a good exercise to regularly examine your profit and loss statements, pondering each and every trade to determine when it was made, why it was made, and your state of mind before, when and after it was made. This will help unlock your individual trading patterns. If you are systematically wrong and you know why you did what you did, all you will have to do is the opposite. Some common trading patterns might be being constantly early or constantly late; taking profits and/or losses too slowly or too quickly; or essentially what you do, and how you do it. Look for what you did well and what you did not do so well. Again, look at the results, and always try to improve.

Being Early

We have considered that time regulates price promotion activity and that risk is a function of price and time, not just price. (Knowing this, we will soon consider the logical necessity for weighting trades.) Indeed, understanding time is the last key element standing in the way of achieving a sound trading strategy, and will probably be the key to improving your trading pattern. Specifically, few trader/investors consider:

1. The concept of their individual timeframe.
2. Whether or not it differs from the timeframe they are trading from.
3. Whether or not it differs from the timeframe they are expecting results in.

In other words, most traders could benefit from considering the timeframe their situation and personality are best suited to, the timeframe they are trading from, and comparing that to the timeframe during which they expect the market to move in their favor.

Curing the Trader's Biggest Problem

As mentioned in the previous chapter, the biggest mistake people make in any endeavor is hesitating and thus being late. It is the same in trading and investing. We all face a natural human tendency toward lateness. The adage "buy low, sell high," can easily turn into the opposite for those participants who have the problem of chronic lateness.

Being late is caused by the natural tendency to hesitate, compounded by the fact that in markets, usually the best decision is the one most difficult to make, as it often flies in the face of activity in the immediate past. Humans hesitate to be "sure" and thus more comfortable, rather than being impulsive, alone and uncomfortable. Another factor that greatly adds to the propensity to hesitate lies in the fact that most situations are very competitive and the opportunity itself isn't so obvious.

The Goal of Every Market Participant

In any decision-making process, an unenunciated timing spectrum exists. In other words, assuming an objective "best time to implement" point exists, the decision can be implemented on a time spectrum ranging from very early to early to on time, on time to late and then very late.

To ask yourself to consistently be on time is to be unrealistic, because great opportunities offer a small window during which to act, and timing entry into that window perfectly is a rare occasion for most. This problem can be neutralized if you design early indicators, signals that will allow you to hesitate and still be able to time the trade so as not to be late. This is extremely important in competitive instances where the majority of indicators are not clear-cut, but are perceived as invisible. In other words, the majority of individuals must be satisfied to adjust their timing to compensate for their humanity. They must be satisfied being nearly on time most of the time and being perfectly on time only occasionally.

Most individuals can adjust by aiming for the "early to on time" area rather than the "on time" area in the timing spectrum. This insight displays an understanding that planning to be early will not always translate into being early, given that human tendencies toward hesitation will often cause an individual to lose time in the decision-making process anyway.

Implementing this means taking two actions: first of all, concentrate on buying breaks and selling rallies most of the time rather than vice versa. Secondly, concentrate on acting in the market alone, being in step with the market and monitoring and trading the market in your timeframe.

Some Myths on Risk

While your trading strategy is dependent on your market understanding as it relates to your needs and abilities, it is also intimately tied to your assumptions about risk. Consider several false assumptions which exist concerning risk in markets and risks associated with taking action in them. Consider specifically how each of these false assumptions tends to reinforce a losing trading strategy.

The first false assumption illustrates the importance of combining a market understanding with a conservative trading strategy before taking action in a market. It is widely promulgated that liquid markets, particularly the futures markets, exist because they enable someone who doesn't feel comfortable holding a position in the market to be able to transfer his risk to someone who will take the risk in hopes of reaping speculative profits. Hence, it is said, an organized exchange provides a vehicle for risk transfer where every participant who is not relieving himself of risk is taking on risk.

However, informed participants who have a cohesive approach to the market grounded in a strong market understanding, and expressed in a solid trading strategy, really assume no risk over a large sample size of transactions. Thus, knowledge reduces risk. If an informed participant does not have a strong market understanding on any one trade, he disciplines himself so that he doesn't make the trade. Thus, knowledge plus discipline eliminates risk over the large sample size.

While over a large sample size, there is no risk transfer for the informed participants, risk is transferred to the uninformed, undisciplined majority — those without a market understanding who inevitably lose. Thus, those with a market understanding and a cohesive approach have a risk profile similar to the gaming companies that operate casinos in the world's major gambling resorts, or to large, well-managed insurance underwriters. In other words, while risk is assumed for the small sample size — every individual transaction — risk of loss is factored out over the large sample size.

(In the casino example, the customer receives entertainment and the short-term possibility of winning money, while the gaming company which owns and operates the casino receives a profit over the large sample size. Since both sides receive value, regardless of loss to the customer or profit to the casino, a zero-sum situation does not exist. Likewise, insurance underwriters provide a risk transference vehicle and peace of mind for individuals while making a profit over the long term, again negating the zero-sum argument. Futures markets clearly are not zero-sum games, any more than casinos or insurance companies are.)

This brings us to an important realization: In any market, and especially the futures market, informed participants who have a cohesive approach to the market grounded in a strong market understanding, and expressed in a solid trading strategy, cannot be considered equal to other participants, since they really assume no risk over a large transactional sample size. In other words, every participant who is not relieving himself of risk is by necessity taking risk over the large sample size.

Thus, contrary to the findings of the academic community, "beating the market," the much sought-after dream of every investor-trader, is in fact possible. Of course, anyone who reads the popular financial press knows not only that beating the market is possible, but in fact exists, since there are numerous very successful market participants. But beating the market is now in fact very possible for a significant portion of formerly unsuccessful participants with the promulgation and application of the principles contained in this book. Beating the market is done merely by trading and/or investing from the posture that most well-thought-out and well-managed businesses assume, using the principles most people unconsciously apply in unorganized markets. In other words, if a person can get strong in each of the areas on the left-hand side of the equation for results, he will be in the situation where his market participation will be profitable over the long term. At this point, he will essentially be winning on the grind much like the casino or the insurance underwriter.

A second false assumption about risk is reflected in the notion that the greater the risk, the greater the potential reward. Nothing could be more completely false, particularly when viewed over a large sample size. The more risk you take, the less you will make, again, especially over a large sample size.

To illustrate, consider the example of the risk associated with purchasing a used car. In the first scenario, a mechanic is aware of the condition of the car and knows that it is worth $2000. If he can buy it for $1000 at a bankruptcy sale, he is taking virtually no risk, yet he should make a very substantial percentage return.

Contrast this to a second scenario: an auction situation where the buyer is not a mechanic (and hence is not in a strong position to evaluate the car's condition and value). Assume further that he gets emotionally excited and purchases the same car for $1800, thinking he can sell it for $2000. The auto purchaser's risk is in fact much greater in this second scenario, yet his potential for profit is much smaller.

The third false assumption about risk: viewing a potential market opportunity in terms of a risk-reward ratio is the wrong way to assess risk. An example is the buyer who purchases hoping to receive 4x in profit, but vowing to get out if the market falls to a level where he would lose x first. This strategy is implicit in the previously mentioned common losing trading strategy which relies on the use of stop-loss orders.

Market exposure and risk tolerance should not be predicated on price alone but always on a combination of price and time. In other words, risk is a function of time. Thus, the risk of every opportunity should be analyzed from the standpoint of how much time one has before one must exit the particular trade, as mentioned in the discussion of combinations. This is following a well-thought-out investment strategy wherein the investor purchases below value and holds over time. The more time one has in which to hold the purchase and make a decision, the more data one can look at and the less risk one is exposed to.

To illustrate, the person who absolutely has to sell his car today because he needs the money is a short timeframe seller and is not in as strong a bargaining position as the fellow who does not have to sell under pressure, but can do so at any time over the next six months, waiting for the best offer. In the latter example, risk is reduced whereas in the former, risk is enhanced and an emotionally motivated decision is likely. When initiating a position, one must consider how much time one has to hold the trade and make a decision on whether to take a loss, make a profit, or break even.

The Importance of Weighting Trades

Now that several myths on risk have been debunked, consider some practical implications: Given that all prices and hence all market opportunities are not the same — some are more attractive than others — and given the falseness of the third false assumption of risk, namely that risk should be handled as if it were a function of price rather than a function of price and time, and finally, given that as individuals, we function at different levels of effectiveness at different times, the results-oriented participant who understands all of these can now begin to formulate strategy. He monitors the market and himself, distinguishes between very attractive, attractive, and average situations and weights the size of his position accordingly.

If you can differentiate between opportunities, assess risk, then weight trades properly, you will have a better win-loss record on what are categorized as the most attractive positions than on what are categorized as the everyday opportunities. This puts you in a position where year-end results are better than your overall trading average. In other words, if each trade is recorded as either a win or a loss, your overall win-loss record for the year will be a lower percent than your win-loss record for what are perceived to be the lowest-risk trading opportunities, which are more heavily weighted, or larger sized positions. Weighting trades puts the participant in a position where he does not have to make an exceptional percentage of correct decisions, since on the large positions, which will make the major results, there are only a few decisions to make. For example, over a small sample size, a coin can be flipped and come up heads three times in a row. Likewise, a sample of three big trades can have the same exceptional decision rate.

Consider the strategy of trading three different sized positions: an everyday small position, a medium sized position where one has some conviction and thus can hold the trade over time, and the maximum position, which is initiated only when the lowest risk, most attractive opportunities occur. The strategy of weighting trades is built around the goal of never being wrong when holding a maximum position, thus boosting year-end results to a higher level than the win-loss record.

When the market is undervalued over the very short term, in a situation where you do not have any conviction as to where value is moving other than in the shortest timeframe, only a small-sized position should be entered. Thus, in a situation where a loss of capital can occur from entering and holding a position and suffering exposure, and being wrong, only a small-sized position should be initiated. In other words, with the smallest sized exposure, you are paying $1.50 for something that you think is going to $2.00, but which is only worth a dollar. A small monetary loss of this nature cannot be held, since the participant does not have time working in his favor if he is wrong. In this type of situation, you must react to what the market is doing immediately when taking a small loss, and not wait to consider.

When the market is undervalued over the long and medium term, but perhaps overvalued over the very short term, a medium-sized position should be entered on the buy side. Thus, in a situation where you have enough time to get out without a loss -- since time is on your side -- after entering and holding a position, suffering exposure, and being wrong, a medium-sized position should be initiated. In other words, with a medium-sized exposure, you are buying something worth a dollar and paying a dollar for it. You have lower risk than in a small position because you have both a longer period of time to exit the trade and a larger profit potential. However, it is very important to have a strong market understanding over both the short term and the medium term before entering the market with a medium-sized position.

When the market is undervalued over the very long timeframe, undervalued over the medium timeframe, and undervalued in the short timeframe, a maximum position should be entered on the buy side. Thus, you should initiate a maximum position only when you can enter the market, hold the position and suffer exposure, realize that you are wrong, and still get out with a profit. In other words, with a maximum position, you should be buying something for 50 cents that is worth a dollar. So long as you can continue to hold the position, you cannot lose, assuming conditions remain unchanged. Just because the market falls to 45 cents doesn't mean you have to sell, nor do you as it goes to 55 cents. The participant can hold the position through time with minimal risk, because price is far under value from a long timeframe perspective. Indeed, the market may fall and the maximum position can show a loss, but this should not be a major concern. It is a loss you do not have to take, since maximum positions should be very long timeframe trades initiated only after it is clear that the long timeframe participants are finally entering the market opposite a long-term trend.

It should be noted that the window of time where such an attractive opportunity occurs and you are trading very well at the same time does not occur every day for most participants, but rather only a few times a year.

Don't Predict, Visualize

Experienced traders and investors summon the courage to take action, yet they never seem surprised when the unexpected occurs and they are forced to retreat. This is because they are prepared for the unexpected because they visualize all the possibilities.

It is very important to visualize the many ways in which the market may unfold, rather than trying to forecast or predict how it will unfold. With a market understanding, you can begin to visualize each possibility, and what each would indicate to you about the market and your position. Visualizing the possible ways in which reality can unfold will mean that the market will bring no surprises. Training yourself to visualize also allows you to be prepared so that you can be early. Furthermore, once you begin operating from reality, you cannot be surprised and can be comfortably early; expectations and hesitation no longer are unmanageable problems.

A sound trading strategy is one in which the participant trades value and the market's current structure, not the last price. Structure is the range of opportunity offered to the marketplace whereupon values are developed and rejected. The futures markets structure is illustrated by a normal distribution profile. [9]

In the final analysis, always consider what your strategy really is. Are you continually buying rallies, or are you buying breaks? Are you reacting to the promotional ability of price, or are you reacting to an advertised opportunity? Learn how to be independent, think for yourself, have conviction to put understanding into action. Have the ability to think and the courage to apply your thinking at the right time, namely, when you are early.

When all else fails, it might be helpful to try executing a series of trades with the express goal of losing some capital. If this approach is successful, simply do the opposite with an equal series, and you should be on the road to consistent profits.

---

[9] The CBOT Manual illustrates five basic structural types of range development which can be used to classify the present situation. Knowing a market's structure-type is important in that it can allow one to identify within a few hours the types of structure one is working with. This moves the individual's information from happenstance to

relative certainty after only a short period of developed market activity. The author's have decided not to recreate this data for reasons of space, but highly recommend it to those interested in pursing an understanding of market-generated activity.

15

CONCLUSIONS

Y our "net worth" really is your ability to function, nothing more. Once a person has the ability to function, faith in himself and his ability to handle all situations, and finally the discipline to do what he has decided he must do, financial statements no longer hold so great a meaning. Man moves into a mode where he is self-sufficient. At this point, nothing material is of importance, simply because any goal worth working toward will not be out of reach for long. Each of us must integrate this into our thinking if we are to approach any market from a nonemotional, consistently logical manner.

This reflection is mentioned and addressed to the many individuals who are attracted to financial markets because they believe that making money as an independent trader or investor is relatively easy and they equate money with success. Both of these beliefs are false. Making money in business almost always entails substantial struggle. Further, producing positive results in any business does not necessarily yield success. Success is being happy; it results when you do what you want to do, because you want to do it. When you are glad to be you, and you have freedom and happiness, then and only then are you successful. Success is especially not found by making more money than the next person, and it is a rare person with such an attitude who is able to both make money and be happy. The participant who trades to make money as a means of proving his worth to himself and others can expect many problems along his journey.

The authors have had the benefit of exposure to many individuals who have garnered media attention because of their conventional success in financial markets. Yet true success lies in fulfilling your potential -- doing the best you can do, being the best you can be. Thus, the authors would widen the class of "the best" investors and traders beyond those who have made many millions.

With such a definition, the best investors and traders, as a class, have an attitude of charity and generosity toward their fellow man. A jealous person has a very hard time succeeding in a marketplace, as he is always reacting emotionally, rather than logically. The best participants tend not to be affected when someone is performing better than they. Indeed, you should be happy when your fellow man is doing well. This ties in with a dilemma: on the one hand, strive to be glad to be who and what you are. On the other hand, develop a humility and strive to control your ego. It is very difficult to fulfill your potential as a trader if you have what might be termed a large ego. In other words, don't have ego represent something you are not and don't be afraid to be you. Either problem may end in stubbornness and the inability to own up to a mistake.

Another outlook which typifies the best trader involves the realization that there always will be those who have greater talents. He is not bothered by outwardly competitive instincts, nor is he seeking a feeling of supremacy through his market involvement. The best trader acknowledges that no one can be the best in a qualitative sense, since being the best is a personal matter. Thus, being the best is really a non-issue to the enlightened participant. Rather than competing against others, the best trader channels his competitive instincts inwardly. In other words, the superior outlook for a trader does not include striving to be the best, but rather striving to be the best he can be.

Once an individual truly accepts this point, he can begin to view markets in a greater context, and the importance of each decision is put into proper perspective, and hopefully decisions come easier and less stressfully. The paradox of the financial world is that only when you are glad to be you do you have freedom, happiness and the ability to attain success easily.

Management

This book has introduced many concepts which fly in the face of the current conventional wisdom on markets. Yet, it is not so radical as one might think. What the authors advocate is little more than thinking logically about markets and applying to trading and investing the common management techniques used in all other business endeavors.